nobu miami

nobu miami
THE PARTY COOKBOOK

Nobu Matsuhisa
Thomas Buckley

FOREWORDS BY
Daniel Boulud and Ferran Adrià

PHOTOGRAPHS BY Masashi Kuma

KODANSHA INTERNATIONAL
Tokyo • New York • London

Distributed in the United States by Kodansha America Inc., and in the United Kingdom and continental Europe by Kodansha Europe Ltd.

Published by Kodansha International Ltd., 17–14 Otowa 1-chome, Bunkyo-ku, Tokyo 112–8652, and Kodansha America Inc.

First edition, 2008
17 16 15 14 13 12 11 10 09 08   10 9 8 7 6 5 4 3 2 1

Library of Congress Cataloging-in-Publication Data

Matsuhisa, Nobuyuki.
  Nobu Miami : the party cookbook / by Nobu Matsuhisa and Thomas Buckley ; photographs by Masashi Kuma ; forewords by Daniel Boulud and Ferran Adria.
      p. cm.
  Includes index.
  ISBN 978-4-7700-3080-1
  1. Cookery, Japanese. 2. Entertaining. 3. Nobu Miami (Restaurant) I. Buckley, Thomas, chef. II. Title.
  TX724.5.J3M338 2008
  641.5952--dc22
                              2008022586

www.kodansha-intl.com

CONTENTS

FOREWORD

All Nobu's restaurants have his signature Japanese style, but each has a unique personality thanks to its particular chef and location. *Nobu Miami* is a perfect example of this sprit of collaboration. The restaurant reflects the energy of Executive Chef Thomas Buckley and the beautiful city of Miami.

Thomas worked for me for many years at Restaurant Daniel in New York. He has amazing creativity, a passion for cooking and great technical talent. What impresses me most about Thomas is that he is a British chef trained in the classic French tradition, who has lived in America for over a decade and has embraced Japanese cuisine with such success. I never thought he would leave French food behind, and in many ways he hasn't. As is obvious from the recipes in *Nobu Miami*, he is still very fond of traditional French techniques (he confits his duck, braises his octopus, and makes his *alfajores* with classic sablé biscuits) and French ingredients (*foie gras* makes a few appearances and the humble *poussin* is paired most unusually with wasabi sauce!). I was also delighted to find that some favorite American dishes serve as inspiration, as in the "Toro Pastrami"—cold smoked tuna belly rubbed with peppercorns, paprika, coriander and garlic, sliced thin and served with *yuzu* ponzu.

Nobu Matsuhisa is of course incredibly worldly, his empire spanning the globe from Los Angeles to Australia, with stops in Italy, the Greek isles, and Hong Kong. His food is firmly anchored in Japanese tradition, but is also always enhanced by the tastes, aromas, colors, and textures of his travels. In *Nobu Miami*, Nobu puts his own personal stamp on many classic dishes from all corners of the world, including *arroz con pollo* (but in this version, with shellfish), a carpaccio (of octopus), and most creatively, a mojito (with *uni*).

Miami entertaining has a style all its own. There is a cool casualness in approach and a real zest for living that gets translated into the city's cooking. Nobu's food naturally has a bit of an island feel that makes it fit right in here. He takes beautiful basic ingredients—freshly harvested shellfish or newly ripened tropical fruits—and introduces them in sharp contrast to each other. He never over-thinks presentation, but his plates always look gorgeous. Nobu knows that the simplest things can be the most stunning. Not surprisingly, I was amazed by the beauty of the pictures in this book, from the technicolor scales of snapper and coralfish to the brilliant pinks of thinly sliced watermelon radishes and the simple sight of a row of boats resting in a sunny harbor. Miami is a beautiful backdrop for Nobu and Thomas's extraordinary food, both at their restaurant and in this exciting book.

Daniel Boulud —Daniel

Throughout the years, many cooks have shared their expertise in the kitchen at my restaurant, elBulli. The list is extensive; however, if I had to name those who left their mark and made a difference at elBulli, it would become much shorter. I would definitely have to include Thomas Buckley in such a list, as he had a great impact and is fondly remembered by the restaurant team. Thomas is remarkable not only for his professional skills, which are of the highest order, but also for his personal qualities as a co-worker and a team player. As anyone who has worked for me knows, this element is highly valued at elBulli.

Thomas has such attributes in abundance. I remember that he became a key element of our team during the time that he worked at the restaurant. His presence on our team was undoubtedly an important factor in the success we enjoyed that season. I also remember stopping by Nobu Miami with Ramón Andrés during the Food and Wine Festival of 2006. It is very important to me to follow the careers of those who have worked for me at some point, and on that occasion I was enormously pleased to see that Thomas had exceeded all his professional expectations, and had gone above and beyond his goals.

For these reasons, I feel honored to contribute these lines for the book that Thomas has written with the highly esteemed Nobu Matsuhisa. I have always maintained that Nobu's cooking has had an enormous influence on the gastronomic world, particularly because he has brought together a range of different influences to create a brilliant nexus of culinary traditions. This is reflected in the character of Nobu's restaurants, as well as in Thomas Buckley's *savoir faire* and great personality. With this in mind, I encourage all admirers and followers of fine food to "devour" this book with all five senses.

Ferran Adrià —elBulli

INTRODUCTION

Twenty-one years have passed since I first opened Matsuhisa in Los Angeles and fourteen since the opening of Nobu in New York. Now, with over twenty-one restaurants around the world, I'm constantly rushing from place to place.

People say I'm a success. Well, if money and fame were everything, I'd have to agree, though of course life's not so simple. I don't spend my days just checking sales figures and making media appearances.

Much more significant for me are times like when I first I visited Cape Town, where I went into a restaurant and there on the menu were Soft Shell Crab Roll, Yellowtail Sashimi with Jalapeño and Nobu-style Saikyo Miso . . . Nobu signature dishes all. I knew my original creations had become standards in many American restaurants, but I never dreamed they had traveled all the way to South Africa! My first encounter with Nobu cuisine "overseas" came as a great surprise. Did being imitated like that make me angry? Not at all. I was overjoyed to see these items on the menu.

Likewise, when I look across the sushi bar and see customers beaming great big smiles, I feel totally fulfilled. No matter how far away they're sitting, I can read an expression that says "delicious." I always put my heart and soul—my *kokoro*—into every dish I make, so whenever I see a happy customer I can say with complete satisfaction, "I'm so glad I'm a chef."

I enjoy cooking in front of customers. It's probably the sushi chef in me. Nothing pleases me more than joking and talking while I cook, making sure that everyone's happy. So preparing food in the spotlight at live events and parties always brings out my vital creativity!

When one of my partners came to me with the idea of opening a Miami restaurant, as always, my first thought was to check the place out for myself, so I flew right over from LA. The area called South Beach, with its white sands, became an immediate favorite. Here the sea reflects a perfect blue sky, turning from green to ultramarine moment by moment. The palm trees could be in LA or Hawaii, but the streamlined curves of the Art Deco buildings really make this town unique.

Florida is one of America's treasure troves for fishing. The mere mention of spiny lobster or conch shells elicits drools from anyone who knows seafood. The fish here is fresh, firm and meaty, the tastes clean and pure. There's citrus aplenty, and tropical fruit from the Caribbean and South America is easy to get. Our Nobu restaurants take pride in sourcing only the best seasonal ingredients—and nothing could be easier in Miami. So even when serving up Nobu standards here, we make every effort to use local ingredients—whether at the restaurant or catered parties.

This book brings together the most popular party foods from Nobu Miami. In this cocktail party city, that typically means bite-size finger food. All very casual, all best eaten with a glass in one hand, allowing everyone to move about and mingle. Unlike a sit-down dinner, this style of dining doesn't tie people to any one fixed spot.

Of course, we do include pass-around pastas, slice-and-share lamb racks, foods that practically float across the table from hand to hand—friend to friend, parent to child, host to guest. They are the life of a party. Nothing too fancy, just a casual spread to bring people closer together.

And because Miami also loves semi-formal dinner parties, these recipes feature some extravagant ingredients and hidden dramatic surprises. Basically "Nobu Style" inspirations, they can be just as enticing plated in single-serving portions.

These Nobu classics, party cocktails and desserts all have zing with a Florida twist. Each recipe is simple, yet can be adapted as you like using your own local ingredients. But remember, no dish can be completed just by following a recipe. Only when you add *kokoro* will your cooking truly become delicious and really please people. That's right—your heart, or *kokoro*, is your own special touch.

I couldn't think of any better chef for Nobu Miami than Thomas Buckley. Whenever I went to London, I'd always talk business with Mark Edwards, Executive Chef at Nobu London, but just by looking at Thomas hard at work back in the kitchen, I could tell he and I shared the same vision. He is a man of few words, but for me it's better to be able share feelings without talking. Thomas simply resonates professional *kokoro*—that was the biggest factor. Naturally, business sense plays a big role, too, and in that department he also has a sure grasp of the Nobu brand, a keen ability to source prime ingredients and great leadership skills. While his own cooking shines with creativity, he doesn't pretend to know it all; he listens to everyone from top to bottom—and that's very important.

Thomas first learned the basics through French cuisine, then gained lots of experience at *stages* around the world. A wonderful person, he's brought a fresh new taste to Nobu.

I come from a completely different background in cooking. Right from the start I realized that Japanese and South American cultural flavors would be full of new things for him, but seeing Thomas in London, and how honestly he accepted my ideas, I knew he had the potential to really blossom. Even today, he shows an amazing passion for learning about Japanese and South American foods.

Ultimately, the bottom line is that Nobu cuisine is essentially Japanese; it comes from where I come from. Thomas has to make use of everything he's done up to now and make it fit with what's basic to me. It's a thrill to see a foreigner try to work out my cooking.

There are all different walks of people in my kitchens. Maybe not quite a meeting of cultures, but we definitely try to understand each other *kokoro* to *kokoro*—it's a natural everyday thing in the kitchen.

A chef's state of mind always shows in the taste of the food. Cooking professionals speak of "authorities" who surround themselves with techniques and traditions they alone understand. Such "authorities" demand way too much respect, if you ask me. My cooking has none of that "this is mine alone" attitude; nothing is "impossible for others to make." Just as I myself have been influenced by many people, the more everyone at Nobu encounters and exchanges ideas and influences with others, the more our Nobu flavors evolve. Within that process, we naturally create new signature dishes that people come to know and love. That's why Nobu cuisine has lasted so long and appealed to so many different people the world over.

Lately, when I ask myself, "Nobu, are you really a success?" my *kokoro* answers, "No, you still haven't quite succeeded as a person." So many people have given me opportunities up to now, and I'd like to give chances to as many others as I can.

Among the many Nobu staff now working in different parts of the world, some are bound to surpass me. I can hardly wait. It's perfectly okay to start by imitating how I cook, but when someone improves on a Nobu dish, it pushes me to try even harder. As one effort goes beyond another, only the best survive to get passed on. As I see it, people have always trained the next generation, but being able to actively influence each other across generations like this is ideal.

So, no, I'm not thinking to retire any time soon. I've still got a long way to go before I'm convinced in my *kokoro* that I've succeeded as a person.

Nobu Matsuhisa

A Few Thoughts

I was helping out in the pastry section of Nobu Park Lane in London when Executive Chef Mark Edwards informed me that Nobu was opening a new outpost in Miami. Would I like to go?

Well, why not!

Miami doesn't feel like the U.S. With its blend of Hispanic and Afro-Caribbean culture, it is an extension of South America and the Caribbean islands. The influences are felt in everyday life, and with the sunshine, beaches, great fishing and local hospitality it is easy to see why people like it here.

Latin people like to feast and feast late! At Nobu Miami we are sometimes cooking and serving until the early hours, for Miami is also a fun destination where living *la vida loca* is a way of life! It seemed almost a given that we base the new cookbook on Nobu Miami's festive party scene, with its elegant settings, sophisticated parties and vibrant atmosphere.

For a chef from Europe, cooking in Miami is exciting in the array of new produce and seafood that can be found. The only problem is that it can be hard to follow the seasons—it's usually hot or very hot with some rain in between!

The essence of Nobu's cuisine is Japanese, but now, with many restaurants spanning the world, a certain globalization has taken place and the cuisine is influenced by region, culture and of course the abundant indigenous produce found in each location. At Nobu Miami, the food tends to be a little spicier, because in the tropics, spice encourages perspiration, which helps regulate the body's temperature—so lay on the chili!

In this cookbook we return to Nobu Matsuhisa's first culinary adventures in Peru and South America and revisit some of the ingredients, find new items and portray them in the now-famous "Nobu Style"—the freshest ingredients, prepared simply with a Japanese ethic and style. For this book, we also play with traditional dishes and re-invent them in our style.

Our cuisine is very spontaneous, and a lot of dishes are custom made to suit a particular customer or menu. We recommend that you follow this approach in these recipes: change around the sauces, mix and match, see what goes with what, and above all, see what tastes good.

Most of the recipes are simple, with ingredients that can be found through a quick search on the Internet or a visit to your local Asian grocery store. Many of the ingredients can be replaced with similar substitutes (for example, Florida fish can be replaced with a local variety).

Above all, enjoy, have fun and cook with your *kokoro*!

¡Fiesta!

Thomas Buckley

FINGER FOODS

BAKED EGGPLANT WITH KINZANJI MISO

In Japan, skewers of tofu or eggplant brushed with sweet miso and grilled over a low flame are called *dengaku*. Here's the Nobu version: tender, thin-skinned Japanese eggplants are baked and topped with Kinzanji miso, sesame and orange peel. A fermented mixture of rice, soybeans, barley and assorted vegetables with a lovely balance of sweet and sour, Kinzanji miso isn't used for seasoning or miso soup, but as a condiment for rice or a soft-ripened cheese-like nibble alongside drinks. Almost any good miso, however, will work with this recipe—try more readily available yellow miso sweetened to taste with a little sugar and *mirin* cooking sake. Delicious! —*N.M.*

MAKES 12 TO 16 PIECES

4 Japanese eggplants
2 tbsp. sake
3 tbsp. Sake Soy (recipe follows)
6 to 8 tsp. Kinzanji miso
Zest from 1 orange, finely shredded
1 tsp. sesame seeds

1. Preheat the oven to 380 °F (190 °C).

2. Cut the eggplants into rounds about 1 in. (2.5 cm) thick and place in water to prevent discoloration. Drain and blot dry. Place onto a half sheet pan and sprinkle with the sake and Sake Soy.

3. Bake until slightly soft. Remove and place ½ tsp. Kinzanji miso on each piece. Return to the oven and bake a further 3 to 4 minutes.

4. Place a little orange zest on each round and sprinkle with the sesame seeds. Serve warm.

SAKE SOY   MAKES SCANT 1 CUP (220 ML)

⅔ cup (160 ml) sake
5 tbsp. soy sauce

Bring the sake to a boil in a saucepan and immediately remove from heat. Cool to room temperature. Combine with soy sauce.

DUCK "SUSHI" WITH YAKUMI CONDIMENTS

Harking back to Nobu's days making sushi in Peru, this *nigiri-zushi* uses lozenges of fried potato in place of the more typical *shari* "rice" base. The humble potato is a native pre-Columbian staple, as central to the Peruvian diet as rice is to that of Japan. If you can't find Peruvian yellow potatoes, then go for russet or any all-purpose fluffy baking potatoes. Along with wasabi, here the *yakumi* condiments are grated ginger, minced scallions and *momiji oroshi*—grated daikon radish mixed with red chili. Just a little of each goes a long way to bring out the sweet richness of the duck meat and cleanse the palate of any fatty aftertaste.

—T.B.

MAKES 12 PIECES

1 duck breast, trimmed
Shichimi spice powder
Salt and pepper
2 medium Peruvian yellow potatoes, peeled
Duck fat for frying potatoes (at least 1 cup / 200 g)
2 tsp. grated wasabi root
1 tbsp. Honey Soy Reduction (recipe follows)
2 tsp. thinly sliced scallion
2 tsp. grated ginger
2 tsp. Momiji Oroshi (p. 183)

1. Score the fat side of the duck breast in a crosshatch pattern, cutting about halfway through the fat. Season both sides with shichimi spice powder, salt and pepper. Heat a sauté pan and put in the duck breast, fat side down. Cook slowly on medium-low heat to render some of the fat and achieve a nice golden color. Turn and cook the other side briefly. Remove the duck breast from the pan and allow to rest.

2. Cut the potatoes into 12 lozenges about 1½ in. (3.75 cm) long by ½ in. (1.25 cm) thick. Rinse and blot dry.

3. Heat the duck fat to 280 °F (140 °C) in a deep saucepan and fry the potatoes in small batches until soft, about 5 minutes. They should be pale but cooked through. Allow them to rest and cool at least 30 minutes as this will help to get rid of a lot of steam, resulting in a crispier potato. Heat the duck fat to 360 °F (180 °C) and refry the potatoes until golden and crisp.

4. Thinly slice the duck breast and place on a paper-lined plate.

5. Dot each potato lozenge with wasabi and place the duck slice on top. Brush with the Honey Soy Reductiom and top with a pinch of Momiji Oroshi, ginger and scallion.

HONEY SOY REDUCTION   MAKES SCANT 1 CUP (210 ML)

½ cup (120 ml) soy sauce
½ cup (120 ml) Acacia or chestnut honey
1 tsp. *kudzu* starch

1. In a saucepan, bring the soy sauce to a gentle simmer. While stirring, add the kudzu starch to thicken. Set aside.

2. Place the honey in another saucepan and heat until warm, then pour into the pan of soy sauce. Place over low heat and simmer gently for 8 minutes, stirring from time to time.

UMAMI SOUP WITH TOMATO AND DASHI

Just as a perfumer retains an encyclopedic memory of scents in order to blend subtle fragrances, it's important for a chef to store up tastes in preparation for creating new flavors. Since working at Nobu, I've gained much more awareness of *umami*. Within the umami spectrum, I always find clear notes of umami in a good, ripe tomato. So it occurred to me: why not combine that with *kombu dashi*, the virtual synonym for umami in Japan? Both are full of glutamic acid, but forget the chemistry—the soup is gorgeous. Once you "get" umami, eating becomes a lot more fun. —*T.B.*

MAKES 16 SHOTS

16 skewers and chilled shot glasses for serving

4 cups (960 ml) Tomato Water (recipe follows)
1 piece dried *kombu*, about 2 in. (5 cm) square
¼ cup (3 g) bonito flakes
4 small *mongo* cuttlefish, mantle only, cleaned and opened
2 *shiso* leaves
2 *yamagobo* pickles, store-bought
16 gingko nuts, blanched

1. Simmer the Tomato Water with the kombu in a pot over low heat for about 40 minutes to extract maximum umami from the kombu. Remove the kombu, and continue to heat until the tomato water is reduced by a quarter.

2. Add the bonito flakes and cool over ice. Strain and keep well chilled.

3. Place the cuttlefish flat, skin-side up, and score the surface at narrow intervals. Flip and lay the shiso leaves and yamagobo pickles on top. Roll the ingredients in the cuttlefish, wrap in plastic wrap to form a tight cylinder, and cook in gently boiling water for 8 minutes. Refrigerate.

4. Pour the tomato water in the glasses. Unwrap the cuttlefish and slice thinly. Thread each slice with a gingko nut on a skewer and rest on the glass as shown.

TOMATO WATER
MAKES 4 TO 6 CUPS (1–1.4 L), DEPENDING ON THE TOMATOES

8 large ripe tomatoes	1 tsp. salt	
2 cloves garlic, crushed	¼ tsp. black pepper	
6 *shiso* leaves	2 tsp. rice vinegar	
2 tsp. brown sugar		

1. Place all ingredients in a bowl and cover with plastic wrap. Set in a warm place or over simmering water for about 20 minutes.

2. Purée all the ingredients in a blender and strain through a sieve lined with cheesecloth.

BLACK GROUPER CHEEKS WITH JAMÓN IBÉRICO AND CAIGUA SALSA

These *pinchos* combine Spanish *pata negra* ham (*jamón ibérico*) with succulent chunks of black grouper cheek poached in sake over a low flame. The concentrated *umami* of the salt-cured ham makes a perfect contrast to the bright, clean taste of the fish. *Caigua* is a hollow, bell pepper-like vine fruit commonly sold in Peruvian markets; its crisp bite makes for an intriguing salsa when combined with red onions and cucumbers. In Peru, caigua is thought to reduce cholesterol, so it goes well with the ham. —*T.B.*

12 skewers for serving

12 grouper cheeks or halibut cheeks (ask your fishmonger to reserve them)
2 tbsp. unsalted butter
¼ cup (60 ml) sake
¼ tsp. salt
Pinch ground black pepper
12 slices *jamón ibérico*
4 tbsp. Caigua Salsa (recipe follows)

1. In a shallow pan, gently simmer the sake to evaporate the alcohol and stir in the butter. Lower the heat and keep the liquid at 125 °F (52 °C). Add the fish cheeks, cover with parchment paper cut into a circle and cook the cheeks in the liquid for 15 minutes. Remove the cheeks from the pan and season with salt and pepper.

2. Wrap the cheeks in the jamón slices, skewer and arrange on a serving platter. Spoon the Caigua Salsa on top. Serve warm.

CAIGUA SALSA

MAKES ABOUT 1½ CUPS (360 ML)

¼ red onion
1 fresh *caigua*, black seeds removed
⅓ Japanese cucumber
½ small red bell pepper, seeded
¼ yellow squash, seeded
½ cup (120 ml) Nobu Ceviche Dressing (p. 38)
1 tbsp. extra-virgin olive oil
2 tbsp. finely chopped cilantro leaves

1. Finely chop the red onion. Cut the caigua, cucumber, red bell pepper and yellow squash into ¼ in. (5 mm) dice. Mix together in a bowl.

2. Combine the Nobu Ceviche Dressing with the olive oil and pour over the vegetables.

3. Just before serving, mix in the chopped cilantro.

UNI TIRADITO NOBU STYLE

One of our signature house dishes with a definite Peruvian accent, the Nobu Tiradito, serves up fresh sashimi with lots of fresh-squeezed *yuzu*, cilantro and *ají rocoto* chilis. We typically make it with white-fleshed fish, but I always wanted to try it with *uni*, so here we roll sea urchin in thin sheets of daikon radish. Sea urchin is very delicate and difficult to handle, but this way you can skewer it or pick it up with chopsticks. Pop one in your mouth, and it's like biting into a ripe fruit as the uni spreads in your mouth. Small but extremely satisfying.   *N.M.*

Melbourne Mule (see p. 188 for recipe)

Melbourne Mule (see p. 188 for recipe)

MAKES 12 PIECES

12 skewers for serving

12 thin sheets of daikon radish, each 2 in. (5 cm) square
12 cilantro leaves
18 pieces *uni* sea urchin (about 6 oz./170 g total)
6 tbsp. fresh *yuzu* juice
2 tsp. Ají Rocoto Vidrio (recipe follows)
Peruvian pink salt or any coarse salt
6 sheets *okiuto* laver (optional)
Garnet amaranth, as garnish (optional)

1. Place a daikon sheet on a cutting board. Put a cilantro leaf in the center of the sheet and top with 1½ pieces (½ oz./15 g) of uni. Spoon 1 tsp. of yuzu juice over. Roll the daikon sheet and spear with a bamboo skewer. Repeat with the rest.

2. Place the okiuto sheets on a serving platter and lay the rolls on top. Dot with the Ají Rocoto Vidrio and sprinkle with sea salt. Garnish with the garnet amaranth.

AJÍ ROCOTO VIDRIO

MAKES 1½ CUPS (360 ML)

8 oz. (240 g) *ají rocoto* (fresh, frozen or paste)
2 tbsp. rice vinegar
4 tbsp. sugar
1 tbsp. olive oil

Place all ingredients in a blender except the oil. Mix to a purée. (If using chili paste, skip this process.) Add the oil little by little while mixing, to form an emulsion.

25

SMOKED TOFU WITH TOMATO, SHISO AND BASIL

Here we take cubes of tofu, marinate them in miso for six hours, and smoke them for ten minutes. This gets rid of the moisture and gives them a texture like semi-hard cheese. Then we peel cherry tomatoes one at a time to complement the firmness of the tofu, and toss with basil and *shiso*. These two herbs are very similar, but have you ever used them together? When combined, they're amazingly fragrant, and make a big impression even in small portions. Tofu and tomatoes, Italian and Japanese herbs—truly an intercultural Insalata Caprese. Serve nice and chilled. —*T.B.*

MAKES 16 PIECES

16 skewers for serving

1 block silken tofu, about 12½ oz. (350 g)
½ cup (120 ml) yellow miso
8 red cherry tomatoes
8 yellow pear tomatoes
2 tbsp. extra-virgin olive oil
1 clove garlic
4 *shiso* leaves, minced
8 small basil leaves, minced
Juice of 1 lemon

Smoking Base
1 tbsp. cherry wood chips
1 tbsp. dry rice

Tomato Jelly Sheets (recipe follows), optional

1. Drain the tofu. Wrap in cheesecloth and spread the miso on all sides. Marinate for about 6 hours. Unwrap and cut into 16 cubes.

2. Heat the wood chips and rice until smoking and place in a metal container with a lid. Place the tofu above the chips on a perforated sheet or rack, cover, and smoke for 10 minutes (do not apply heat). Remove the tofu and set aside.

3. To peel the tomatoes, score a crisscross on the bottom of each tomato, blanch in boiling water for a second and shock in ice water. Remove the skin. Marinate in the mixture of the olive oil, garlic, shiso leaves, basil leaves and lemon juice.

4. Lay a Tomato Jelly Sheet on each serving plate. Skewer together each piece of tofu and a tomato and arrange on top of the tomato sheets.

TOMATO JELLY SHEETS

1 cup (240 ml) Tomato Water (p. 21)
2 tsp. agar-agar powder

Warm the Tomato Water and stir in the agar-agar powder. Cool at room temperature. When it starts to thicken, spread it thinly onto a flat surface, preferably a stainless sheet pan lined with a non-stick silicone mat. When set, cut into 2 in. (5 cm) squares.

CUCUMBER FILLED WITH FLUKE, OLIVES AND WASABI

Japanese cucumber is a favorite ingredient of mine, thin-skinned and wonderfully water-crisp. The only point I need to mention is to cut it on the bias. Slant cuts expose more surface area and make slices easier to stuff or pick up with your fingers. French cuisine often combines cucumbers and fish such as salmon. This finger food gives almost any fish—not just fluke—a healthy boost, flavored only with minced green olives, wasabi and white pepper. Super simple, but simply great. —*T.B.*

Cucumber Martini (see p. 188 for recipe)

Cucumber Martini (see p. 188 for recipe)

MAKES 12 TO 15 PIECES

3 Japanese cucumbers
1 fluke fillet, 4 oz. (120 g), cleaned
2 tsp. extra-virgin olive oil
2 tsp. wasabi paste
6 green olives, pitted and minced
Sea salt
Freshly ground white pepper
Micro *shiso*, as garnish

1. Cut the cucumbers on the bias into slices about 1 in. (2.5 cm) thick. Three cucumbers may yield 12 to 15 pieces. Use a melon baller to scoop out the inside, forming a cup.

2. Dice the fish and mix with the olive oil, wasabi and olives. Season with salt and pepper to taste. Be careful with the salt, as olives can be quite salty.

3. Spoon the fish mixture into the cucumber cups. Arrange on a serving platter and top with micro shiso.

CONCH SHICHIMI

In this Nobu Miami signature dish, we bake conch shells—ours are shipped in fresh daily from the Turks and Caicos Islands—filled with blended butter, very much like *beurre d'escargot à la Bourguignonne*. Only here, we blend the butter with Japanese herbs and spices—*shichimi* "seven-spice pepper," *shiso*, and *mitsuba*—then add a heaping cup of *panko* breadcrumbs and a dash of light soy sauce. The butter-soy sauce combination works incredibly well. (In fact, Matt Damon special-orders his lobster grilled with shichimi butter.) —*T.B.*

MAKES 10 PIECES

10 small conchs, shucked, with the shells reserved
5 tbsp. Shichimi Butter (recipe follows)
1 lemon, cut into halves

1. Using the heel of a knife or a mallet, pound the conch flesh on both sides to tenderize. Spear each conch with a bamboo skewer. Return the flesh to the shell with the skewer upright, and cover with Shichimi Butter.

2. Bake the conch shells in a 400 °F (200 °C) oven for 4 to 5 minutes.

3. Serve with the lemon halves.

SHICHIMI BUTTER

MAKES ABOUT 1 CUP (240 ML)

2 sticks unsalted butter (about 1/2 lb. /225 g)
1 1/2 tsp. garlic purée
10 *shiso* leaves, roughly chopped
1/2 bunch *mitsuba* herb, roughly chopped
1 1/2 tsp. light soy sauce
1 1/2 tsp. *shichimi* spice powder
1/2 cup (30 g) *panko*
1/2 tsp. ground black pepper
1 lemon, separated into zest and juice

Soften the butter and place in a food processor. Add the garlic purée, shiso leaves and mitsuba and pulse until just mixed. Add the rest of the ingredients in sequence and briefly pulse after each addition. Adjust the seasoning with additional light soy sauce if needed .

KING CRAB DAIKON ROLL

Futomaki thick-rolled sushi is a long-standing Nobu signature dish. One day, we got in some ultra-fresh king crab, but instead of using it to top *nigiri-zushi*, we tried making the ultimate thick California roll. No skimping here: we take big chunks of real crab leg, *shiso* and creamy avocado slices and wrap them all in crisp paper-thin sheets of daikon radish. Then we drizzle on our Nobu special jalapeño dressing to really spark the appetite. A very casual snack. —*N.M.*

MAKES 15 PIECES

3 legs king crab, cooked and shelled
3 paper-thin sheets daikon radish, each 8 in. (20 cm) square
6 *shiso* leaves
2 ripe avocados, thinly sliced lengthwise
4 tbsp. Jalapeño Dressing (recipe follows)

Lay a daikon sheet flat. At the front edge of the sheet, layer 2 shiso leaves face side down, a crab leg and avocado slices. Roll up quite tight using a sushi bamboo mat. Repeat with the other two sheets. Cut each roll into 5 pieces with a sharp knife. Arrange on a platter and spoon the Jalapeño Dressing over.

JALAPEÑO DRESSING　　　MAKES ABOUT 1½ CUPS (360 ML)

2 jalapeños, chopped
1½ tsp. sea salt
1 tsp. garlic purée

Scant ⅔ cup (150 ml) rice vinegar
¾ cup (180 ml) grapeseed oil

Combine the jalapeños, salt, garlic and rice vinegar in a food processor and pulse until the jalapeños are finely chopped. Slowly add the grapeseed oil while pulsing until well blended.

POMPANO FLORIDA COCKTAIL

I used to make Florida Cocktail at hotels when I was just starting out in the late 80s. Who'd have thought I'd end up making it in Florida! Now, well into the twenty-first century, we've taken this classic starter to a different level. Here we combine Florida's glorious citrus with another Florida delicacy, pompano, diced up into bite-size pieces. Fresh red chili and pink peppercorns play a surprisingly vital double role in bringing out all the natural goodness and adding colorful accents. —*T.B.*

1 pompano fillet, skinned and diced

2 tsp. extra-virgin olive oil

Pinch minced red chili pepper

2 pink grapefruits

2 oranges

1 tbsp. Ginger Oil (recipe follows)

1 tsp. Peruvian pink salt or any coarse salt

2 tbsp. pink peppercorns, as garnish

Micro cilantro, as garnish

1. Mix the pompano with the olive oil and chili pepper.

2. Cut the skins off the grapefruits and oranges and cut out segments. Juice the remaining pulp and mix the juice with the Ginger Oil. Dice the segments and place on spoons, alternating orange with grapefruit, and place the pompano on top.

3. Sprinkle the spoons with the juice/Ginger Oil mixture and pink salt. Garnish with pink peppercorns and micro cilantro.

GINGER OIL   MAKES ¼ CUP (60 ML)

1 thumb-size knob ginger, peeled

¼ cup (60 ml) grapeseed oil

Place the ginger and grapeseed oil in a saucepan over low heat. When the oil is fragrant but before the ginger changes color, remove from heat. Allow to cool to room temperature.

SPANISH MACKEREL WITH SANSHO CUCUMBER SALSA

Fresh Spanish mackerel is plentiful in Florida. It's very close to what we call *sawara* in Japan and can be used in similar ways. So applying a traditional sushi technique, we first salt the fillets to cut the excess moisture and fishy smell, then douse them in rice vinegar. Both Spanish mackerel and sawara have tender flesh that falls apart easily, but preparing the fish this way makes it easy to handle. Lastly, for a unique touch, we add Sansho Cucumber Salsa. The Japanese appreciate sansho, both the powdered dried berries and the fresh herb sprigs called *kinome*, for the tingling sensation it leaves on the tongue, as well as its subtle bouquet. —*N.M.*

MAKES 12 PIECES

2 fillets Spanish mackerel, ½ lb. (225 g) total, boned
Salt
1 cup (240 ml) rice vinegar
12 large leaves red endive
3 yellow grape or pear tomatoes, quartered
4 tbsp. Sansho Cucumber Salsa (recipe follows)
2 in. (5 cm) length of scallion, white part only, slivered

1. Generously sprinkle the fillets with salt and refrigerate for 15 minutes.

2. Rinse the fillets under cold running water and blot dry. Pour the vinegar into a nonreactive bowl and douse the fillets, turning once, then leave for 5 minutes. The surface of the fillets should turn slightly white. Blot dry (do not wash) and remove thin membrane. Cut into 24 pieces.

3. Arrange 2 mackerel pieces and a tomato quarter on each endive leaf. Add about ½ tsp. of Sansho Cucumber Salsa for each and top with the slivered scallion.

SANSHO CUCUMBER SALSA
MAKES 4 TO 5 TBSP.

½ Japanese cucumber, seeded and finely diced
1 tbsp. finely diced red onion
1 tsp. preserved *sansho* peppercorns, chopped
¼ tsp. chopped *kinome* leaves
1 tbsp. White Ponzu (p. 183)

Combine all ingredients.

BAY SCALLOP AND TOMATO CEVICHE WITH KEY LIME

I love ceviche. I've made it many ways with countless ingredients, but I always keep in mind that ceviche is a simple preparation, so the taste of the ingredients should come straight at you. The citrus element is extremely important. You might think lemon and lime are pretty much the same, but what a difference they make to the taste and texture! Key lime has its own unique concentrated tartness, which adds a special Florida edge to the ceviche. I often crave *limón*, Peruvian lemons; they might look like limes, but they have a refreshing tang that's all their own—an unforgettable flavor. —*N.M.*

MAKES 10 SMALL CUPS

20 fresh bay scallops, in shell, removed from the shell and cleaned

5 small heirloom tomatoes, cut into ½ in. (1 cm) dice

¼ red onion, finely sliced

2 tsp. finely chopped cilantro leaves

3 tbsp. Nobu Ceviche Dressing (recipe follows)

Micro cilantro, as garnish

Mix together the bay scallops, tomato, red onion and chopped cilantro leaves. Combine with the Nobu Ceviche Dressing and let stand for 1 to 2 minutes. Garnish with the micro cilantro.

NOBU CEVICHE DRESSING

MAKES ABOUT ⅔ CUP (160 ML)

2 tsp. *ají amarillo* paste

½ cup (120 ml) key lime juice

4 tsp. *yuzu* juice

2 tsp. soy sauce

1 tsp. garlic purée

1 tsp. grated ginger

1 tsp. sea salt

¾ tsp. freshly ground black pepper

Combine all ingredients.

Pisco Mora (see p. 188 for recipe)

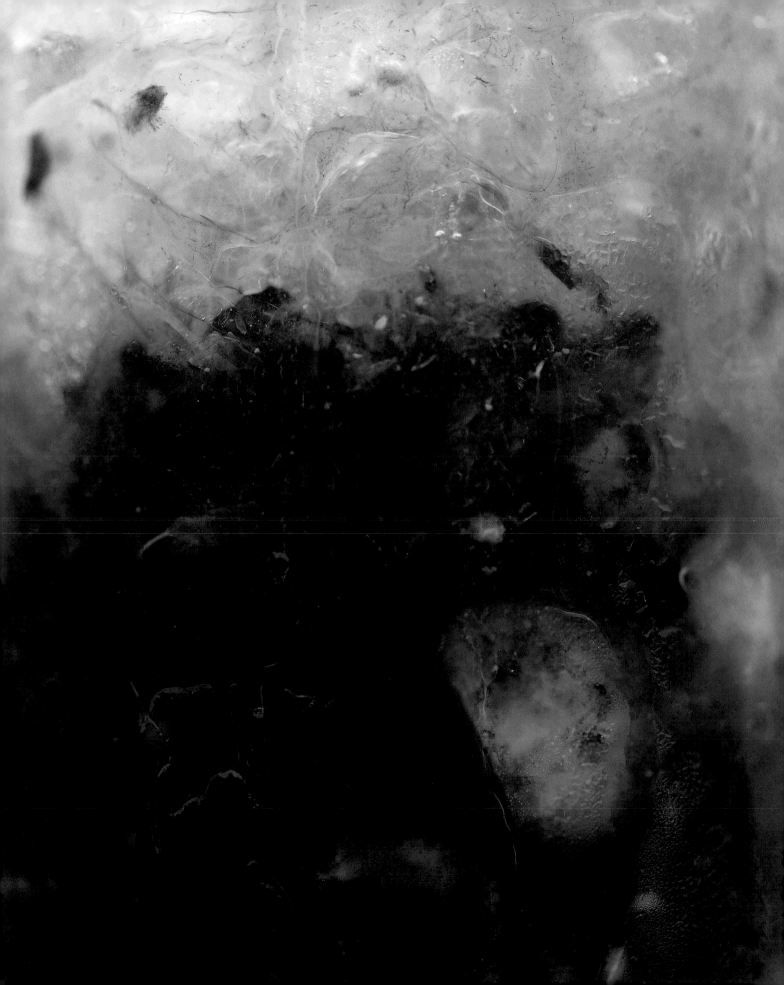

BLACK COD IN BUTTER LETTUCE WRAPS

Here's a Nobu classic that's a big hit at parties. Sear black cod with the skin still on, then slather on Nobu-style Saikyo Miso and grill until fragrant. Serve wrapped in butter lettuce leaves as a finger food. I often do this dish at public tasting events, and even if I make 500 portions, it sells out faster than any other restaurant's offerings. The flavorings are deep and intense, but wrapping in lettuce makes for a light, healthy appeal. —N.M.

SERVES 10

1 to 2 fillets black cod, 12 oz. (340 g) total, skin on, cut into 10 squares

10 tsp. Nobu-style Saikyo Miso (recipe follows)

10 leaves butter lettuce, washed and crisped in cold water

10 pieces Garlic Chips (p. 183)

2 oz. (60 g) frozen *kataifi* dough (shredded phyllo dough), deep-fried

1 thumb-size knob ginger, slivered

1. Sear the skin side of the cod squares under a salamander or broiler. Turn over, spread with the Nobu-style Saikyo Miso and sear until the color changes.

2. Break the Garlic Chips and kataifi dough into each butter lettuce leaf. Top with the cod and slivered ginger.

NOBU-STYLE SAIKYO MISO
MAKES 3 CUPS (720 ML)

⅔ cup (150 ml) sake

⅔ cup (150 ml) *mirin*

1⅔ cups (450 g) white miso

1⅛ cups (225 g) granulated sugar

1. In a medium saucepan, bring the sake and mirin to a boil over high heat to evaporate the alcohol.

2. Turn the heat to low and add the miso, mixing with a wooden spoon. When the miso has dissolved completely, turn the heat up to high and add the sugar, stirring constantly with the wooden spoon to prevent scorching. When the sugar has dissolved completely and the mixture becomes a smooth paste, remove from heat and cool to room temperature.

PERUVIAN PURPLE CHIPS WITH SPICY MISO AND CAVIAR

Complementing sashimi with spicy miso is a special Nobu twist. For that extra note of party *pachanga*, we serve the sashimi slices on potato chips, adding caviar to give just the right saltiness. We use Peruvian purple potatoes for the chips; the trick is not to fry them too hot, or they'll turn brown and lose their festive color. Orange, purple, green—all natural food tones, nothing garish—so the dish looks elegant and appetizing. —*T.B.*

MAKES 12 PIECES

1 purple potato
Salt
4 tuna sashimi slices
4 flounder sashimi slices
4 salmon sashimi slices
4 tsp. caviar (Osetra)
3 tbsp. Kochujan Miso (recipe follows)
12 cilantro leaves
Vegetable oil for deep-frying

1. Slice the potato on a mandoline and rinse immediately in cold water.

2. Heat the oil to 280 °F (140 °C) and deep-fry the slices. They should keep their purple color and not turn brown. Transfer to a paper towel to drain any excess oil. While hot, season with a little salt.

3. Place about ⅓ tsp. of caviar on each fish slice. Roll up and place on a potato chip. Dot the Kochujan Miso on top and garnish with a cilantro leaf.

KOCHUJAN MISO   MAKES 1 GENEROUS CUP (250 ML)

6 tbsp. *kochujan* Korean hot soybean paste
½ cup (120 ml) Den Miso (p. 156)
Scant ¼ cup (50 ml) sake

Combine the kochujan paste and Den Miso, then add sake. Mix well.

Parties come in all different styles, so there's no one definitive party cuisine, but with a tropical cocktail in one hand, "finger foods" come pretty close. The quintessential Japanese finger food is, of course, sushi—which is fine if that's all you're having. But when you want to enjoy a variety of foods, a fishy smell on the fingers might be a problem. In that regard, our House Special Rolls and other Nobu sushi items are perfect for parties. Wrapping the *nori* seaweed with another layer of thinly sliced daikon radish keeps it from sticking to your fingers and leaves a refreshing aftertaste on the palate.

If we are serving soupy foods, we put out flat-bottomed *renge* spoons in a variety of designs. They're good to have on hand in any kitchen. We even had original *renge* spoons made for Nobu restaurants. —*T.B.*

PINCHO DE CAMARON MATSUHISA

ere's a party standard, Matsuhisa Shrimp, served as a *pincho*, or skewered appetizer. Use sashimi-grade shrimp, taking care not overcook them when grilling. The outsides should be tinged white, but the center should remain transparent and half-raw. Wrap each butterflied shrimp (with the white meat showing) around a roasted shiitake mushroom cap and a *shiso* leaf, then secure with a skewer. The saltiness of the caviar and the zest of the *yuzu* are the only seasonings needed. A perfect "little something" for a sea-breezy party on a yacht. —*N.M.*

1. Rinse the shrimp in cold water. Remove the heads and shells, leaving the tails intact. Butterfly by making a slit down the middle of the shrimp on the belly side. Remove the black veins and wipe off any remaining bits with a paper towel (do not wash).

2. Gently grill or broil the shiitake mushrooms and cut into 10 slices.

3. Place a shrimp split-side down on a flat surface and top with a shiso leaf half and a shiitake slice. Roll the shrimp up from head to tail and spear with a bamboo skewer from the tail side. Repeat with the remaining shrimp. Grill or broil for 1 minute until the surface of the shrimp just turns opaque.

4. Arrange on a platter and top each shrimp with caviar. Sprinkle with yuzu juice.

UNI "MOJITO"

Nobu party cocktails include numerous variations on the oyster shooter theme. This one looks southward to the Cuban *mojito* for inspiration, but instead of rum, we use my favorite sake, Hokusetsu, then mix in chopped mint and *shiso*—and of course, it wouldn't be a mojito without lime! It might sound strange, but after one taste you'll agree that sea urchin and mint go surprisingly well together. Just the slightest hint of white soy sauce provides a nice undertaste. —*N.M.*

MAKES 12 SHOTS

Mint-Infused Syrup (makes ⅔ cup / 160 ml)
¼ cup (60 g) granulated sugar
½ cup (120 ml) water
¼ cup (6 g) mint leaves

Nobu Mojito Mix
½ cup (120 ml) lime juice
½ cup (120 ml) Hokusetsu sake
2 tbsp. white soy sauce
¼ cup (60 ml) Mint-Infused Syrup (from above)

9 large pieces *uni* (1½ pieces per shot)
6 large mint leaves, finely chopped
3 *shiso* leaves, finely chopped
6 Cape gooseberries, as garnish

1. Make the Mint-Infused Syrup: In a small saucepan, combine the sugar and water and bring to a boil. Remove from heat and add mint leaves. Cool to room temperature and strain.

2. Make the Nobu Mojito Mix: Measure out ¼ cup (60 ml) Mint-Infused Syrup and combine with the rest of the ingredients.

3. Place uni, mint and shiso into a shot glass. Barely cover with the Nobu Mojito Mix. Cut the Cape gooseberries into halves and garnish each glass with a gooseberry half.

OCTOPUS CARPACCIO WITH YUZU MOJO

The quintessential Cuban *mojo* sauce combines a strong splash of citrus with salt, oil, garlic and onion. Restaurants in Peru often serve Yuca con Mojo, drenching *yuca* or cassava root in this mixture. Of course, for our Nobu-style mojo, we use fresh-squeezed *yuzu*! The garlic and onion are uncooked, which adds a nice water-crisp texture. Here we use the mojo to dress one of Nobu's and my personal favorites—octopus. The prep takes a bit of doing, but I highly recommend this recipe if you really want to enjoy octopus in all its natural jelly-like softness. —*T.B.*

About 5 oz. (140 g) *madako* octopus tentacles

1 daikon radish

Salt

1 piece dried *kombu*, ½ in. (1 cm) square

3 cups mixed salad greens, such as frisée, radicchio or endive

5 tbsp. Yuzu Mojo (p. 183)

1½ tbsp. grated *bottarga*

1. Pound the octopus tentacles with a daikon radish (or wooden mallet, or rolling pin) to tenderize. Salt lightly and rub in a ceramic mortar to get rid of the natural sliminess. Rinse well under cold running water and blot dry.

2. Place the kombu in a pot and add salted cold water to cover the tentacles (2 tbsp. salt to each 1 qt./1 L water). Bring to a gentle simmer. Add the tentacles and cook for 10 to 15 minutes.

3. Remove the tentacles and lay onto plastic wrap. Make sure all the tentacles face in the same direction and tuck in the ends. Roll tightly and close both ends by twisting the plastic wrap like a candy wrapper. Tightly wrap again with aluminum foil.

4. Place the roll in a steamer or in simmering water and cook for 20 to 30 minutes, depending on the thickness of the tentacles. Cool slightly at room temperature and refrigerate for 4 hours so that the natural gelatin of the octopus sets.

5. Unwrap the roll and slice into 20 rounds.

6. Divide the salad greens into individual bowls. Place 2 octopus slices on top and spoon the Yuzu Mojo over. Sprinkle with the grated bottarga.

Living in Peru and Argentina taught me many things: how to liven up sashimi with chili, how to complement tart flavors in ceviche, interesting approaches to raw fish we don't have in Japan. At the same time, I found out the hard way about not having ingredients I took for granted in Japan. That experience gave me strength.

Of all our restaurants, Nobu Miami is the closest to places that influenced me greatly as a chef, which is probably why I feel so nostalgic every time I come to Miami. It takes me back just to hear Spanish spoken in the street.

Miami provides not just wonderful seafood, but all kinds of tropical fruit and chili varieties. Here we get fresh ingredients that are the highlight of what we serve up. Alongside Nobu standards, we've added local flavors that have quickly become hit dishes.

Many celebrities have villas here, and in a flash we were getting orders to cater their parties. Many have visited us in LA or New York, but they look so different here in Miami. Nice and tanned, and totally relaxed in this cocktail atmosphere.

No, Miami isn't your black dress and formal suit kind of place. Mornings start slow in this town—around noon. Everyone's here on vacation, after all! —*N.M.*

KOBE "BURGERS"

These mini-burgers—"sliders" in kitchen lingo—are actually little patties of wagyu beef sandwiched between daikon radish "buns." Wagyu beef or Kobe-style beef is marbled with fat and very rich, so it's flavorful enough in small portions to make a satisfying finger food. The "mustard" and "ketchup" here are Yellow Anticucho sauce and La You Maui salsa. I love playing with classic dishes like this and watching the surprise on people's faces.

—*T.B.*

Strawberry Bloody Mary (see p. 188 for recipe)

MAKES 15 PIECES

15 skewers for serving

"Buns"

1 lb. (450 g) daikon radish
1 cup (240 ml) Dashi Stock (p. 183)
2 tsp. sake
2 tsp. *mirin*
1 tsp. soy sauce

Patties

8 oz. (230 g) ground wagyu beef (about 1 cup)
1 tsp. finely sliced scallion
½ tsp. garlic purée
½ tsp. grated ginger
½ tsp. eel sauce (*kabayaki* sauce)
Pinch salt and ground black pepper

1 tsp. sesame seeds
2 butter lettuce leaves, torn into 15 pieces
5 tsp. La You Maui Salsa (recipe follows)
5 tsp. Yellow Anticucho Sauce (recipe follows)

1. Make the "buns": Peel the daikon and slice into 15 rounds. Cut out circles with a 1 in. (2.5 cm)-diameter ring mold. Bevel the tops of the rounds so that they look like hamburger buns. Place them in a saucepan and fill with cold water to cover. Bring to a boil. Turn off heat and drain. Return the daikon to the pan along with the sake, soy sauce, dashi and mirin. Cook gently until fork tender. Cool in the cooking liquid.

2. Meanwhile, mix the wagyu beef with the scallion, garlic, grated ginger, eel sauce, salt and pepper. Form 15 small patties and refrigerate.

3. Cut the daikon rounds in half, making sure the bottom half is flat so that it will stand on a plate. Remove the patties from the refrigerator and grill. Sandwich lettuce and a beef patty between the daikon "buns" and spear with a skewer. Sprinkle the tops of the daikon "buns" with the sesame seeds.

4. Arrange the burgers on a platter and dot the La You Maui Salsa and Yellow Anticucho Sauce on the side.

LA YOU MAUI SALSA
MAKES SCANT 1 CUP (220 ML)

¾ Maui onion or medium sweet onion, finely chopped
1 medium tomato, skinned, seeded and chopped
6 tbsp. White Ponzu (p. 183)
1 tbsp. fresh orange juice
1 tsp. *la you* hot oil

Combine all ingredients.

YELLOW ANTICUCHO SAUCE
MAKES 1¼ CUPS (300 ML)

8 tbsp. *ají amarillo* paste
5 tbsp. rice wine vinegar
2 tbsp. soy sauce
1 tbsp. lemon juice
1 tbsp. *yuzu* juice
4 tbsp. grapeseed oil

Combine all ingredients except the oil in a blender. Add the oil little by little while blending to emulsify.

KUMAMOTO OYSTERS WITH TORO SALSA

Oysters are just fine with only lemon, but every once in a while, why not try something outrageous, like oysters topped with *toro* tuna belly and caviar? At Nobu we tend to pare things down to minimalist aesthetics, but bite-size tidbits sometimes need extravagant flourishes for impact. The Toro Salsa here blends *tamari* soy sauce, *yuzu* juice, ground yuzu zest-pepper paste and mustard, giving it a fresh citrus zing and a sharp burst of spice that help to tone down the richness of the toro and oyster. —*N.M.*

Toro Salsa

2 oz. (60 g) *o-toro* fatty tuna, diced

1 small white onion, chopped

2 egg yolks, beaten

3 tbsp. olive oil

3 tbsp. *tamari* soy sauce

3 tbsp. *yuzu* juice

¼ tsp. yuzu-pepper paste (*yuzu-kosho*)

¼ tsp. mustard powder

Tengusa sea tangle (optional)

15 Kumamoto oysters, shucked, shells reserved

3 key limes, halved

15 Garlic Chips (p. 183)

1 tbsp. caviar (Osetra)

Chives, cut into 2 in. (4 cm) lengths

1. Make the Toro Salsa: Combine all ingredients and set aside to let the toro marinate until the surface turns slightly white.

2. Lay the sea tangle, if using, on a serving platter, then place the oysters and key lime halves on top. Spoon Toro Salsa onto each oyster. Top with Garlic Chips, caviar and chives.

NOBU-STYLE GRIOT WITH UDO PIKLIS

*G*riot, a Haitian national dish, refers to marinated pork that is boiled off the bone, then fried. Here we season pork in soy sauce, sake and *mirin*, then deep-fry it until the surface turns golden brown. Piklis, or tart pickles, make a great counterpoint to the fatty *kurobuta* pork belly. —*T.B.*

The *udo* (the white twists in the photo) are pungent wild "mountain sprouts" or *sansai*, which are unique to Japan in the spring. Udo is also popular for seasonal springtime tempura. Udo may be hard to find overseas; daikon radish makes a good substitute. —*N.M.*

Miami Margarita (see p. 188 for recipe)

Miami Margarita (see p. 188 for recipe)

MAKES 16 TO 20 PIECES

1 fresh pork belly, 1 lb. (450 g)

Marinade
1 cup (240 ml) soy sauce
1 cup (240 ml) sake
1 cup (240 ml) *mirin*
2 whole star anise
1 tsp. preserved *sansho* peppercorns
½ stick cinnamon, crushed

Piklis
1 carrot, finely sliced
¼ head cabbage, finely shredded
1 white onion, finely shredded
½ *udo* stalk, cut into curls (see recipe for directions)
3 scallions, finely shredded
2 cups (480 ml) rice wine vinegar
1 cup (240 ml) Amazu (p. 183)
4 or more scotch bonnet peppers, cut in half
2 tsp. salt
1 tsp. black peppercorns, crushed

2 tbsp. Rocoto Mustard Miso (p. 183)

1. Make the marinade: Combine the soy sauce, sake, mirin, star anise, cinnamon, and sansho pepper. Marinate the pork for 12 hours.

2. Remove the pork from the marinade, reserving 1 cup (240 ml) marinade. Place the pork into a pot with enough water to cover and bring to a boil. Discard the water, replace it with fresh water and the reserved marinade, and simmer gently for 4 hours.

3. Transfer the pork to a tray lined with plastic wrap. Cover with plastic wrap and place a weight on top. Press overnight.

4. Make the Piklis: Peel the udo in a thin, unbroken strip 1½ in. (4 cm) wide. On a 45° angle, cut the udo into ¼ in. (6 mm) wide strips. Wind the strips around a ½ in. (1 cm) diameter rod and place in ice water until curled and crisp. Mix the udo curls with the other vegetables in a container with a tight-fitting lid. Add the scotch bonnet peppers, rice vinegar, and Amazu and season with salt and peppercorns. Leave overnight to marinate. If you like it hotter, add more scotch bonnet peppers.

5. Trim the pork and cut into strips about ¾ in. (2 cm) wide. Place the strips in a hot pan and fry until crisp on all sides using only the fat that renders out of the pork.

6. Cut the strips into bite-sized cubes and thread onto skewers, as desired. Remove the scotch bonnets from the Piklis and place the Piklis in a serving bowl. Arrange the skewers on top. Dot with Rocoto Mustard Miso.

MUSSELS WITH CITRUS CHILI SALSA

This simple recipe is all about how the mussels are cooked. Typically they're steamed in white wine or other liquid until the shells open, releasing the succulent juices. But here we want all those juices sealed into the flesh of the mussels, and the best way to do that is to parboil them for a mere 15 seconds, then quickly immerse them in cold water and pry open the shells. This barely cooks them through, and leaves the flesh nice and plump. Of course, be sure to select the very freshest mussels you can find. —*N.M.*

10 mussels, cleaned and debearded
3 to 4 tbsp. Citrus Chili Salsa (recipe follows)
10 slices red chili (cut paper-thin)

1. In a medium saucepan, bring plenty of water to a boil. Dip the mussels in, 3 or 4 at a time, and cook for 15 seconds. Plunge into ice water. Open with an oyster knife (this method produces plump, just-cooked mussels).

2. Spoon about 1 teaspoon of Citrus Chili Salsa over each mussel and top with a slice of red chili.

CITRUS CHILI SALSA

MAKES 3 CUPS (720 ML)

1 pink grapefruit
2 limes
1 lemon
1 uniq fruit
1 pomelo
3 Florida oranges
2 tsp. ginger juice from squeezed grated ginger
2 tbsp. Ginger Oil (p. 35)

1 tsp. finely chopped *ají rocoto*
1 tbsp. finely chopped *shiso* leaves
2 tsp. pink peppercorns, crushed
1 tbsp. white soy sauce

2 tbsp. finely chopped cilantro

1. Cut the skin off the grapefruit, cut out segments and dice. Repeat with the limes, lemon, uniq fruit, pomelo and Florida oranges. Combine with all remaining ingredients except the cilantro.

2. Add the cilantro just before serving.

FACING PHOTO: Champagne 95 (see p. 188 for recipe)

BAKED FLORIDA OYSTERS

I've apprenticed in many different countries and I can tell you, the flavor of the same basic items like oysters truly varies from place to place. Traveling along Florida's Gulf Coast, you come upon oyster farms where they raise so-called Eastern oysters (*Crassostrea virginica*), sometimes called "Pensacola oysters," which are very popular along the Eastern Seaboard. I wanted to try giving this local variety a Nobu flair, and the result was these oysters richly glazed with egg yolk, miso, bacon and green apple. The trick is to lightly broil them to bring out that depth of flavor. —*T.B.*

MAKES 10 OYSTERS

10 medium Eastern oysters, shucked, shells reserved
2 cups (2 oz./60 g) baby spinach
1 tsp. olive oil
Salt and pepper
2 tsp. Apple Bacon Miso (recipe follows)
3 tsp. Egg and Tofu Glaze (recipe follows)
3¼ tbsp. micro cilantro, as garnish
10 *yamamomo* bayberry preserves, as garnish (optional)

1. Heat the oil in a frying pan and sauté the spinach, seasoning with salt and pepper. Pat dry with paper towels.

2. Mix the spinach with the Apple Bacon Miso, divide among the oyster shells, and top each with an oyster.

3. Spoon about 1 tsp. of the Egg and Tofu Glaze over each oyster and glaze under a salamander or broiler. Top with the micro cilantro. Arrange yamamomo preserves on the side.

APPLE BACON MISO

MAKES 2 CUPS (480 ML)

6 slices thin-cut bacon
4 green apples, peeled and cut into wedges
1 tbsp. miso
1 tsp. sugar
2 tsp. sake
2 tsp. *mirin*
2 tsp. rice vinegar
2 egg yolks, beaten

2 slices thick-cut bacon
1 green apple

1. In a non-stick frying pan over medium-low heat, fry the thin-cut bacon and render the fat. Continue to cook until crisp. Transfer to a paper-lined dish to drain any excess fat. Break into chunks.

2. Place the apple wedges in a saucepan and add a little water to cover the bottom of the pan. Cook until very soft.

3. Put the miso, sugar, sake, vinegar and mirin in a pan and cook for 10 minutes over low heat, stirring constantly. Cool slightly and add the egg yolks. Add the bacon and cooked apples and transfer to a blender. Blend to a paste. Transfer to a container and leave for 4 hours. Pass through a strainer.

4. Meanwhile, roast the thick bacon slices in a 350 °F (175 °C) oven. Cut into ¼ in. (6 mm) cubes. Peel the apple and cut into ¼ in. (6 mm) cubes.

5. Stir the apples and bacon into the miso just before serving.

EGG AND TOFU GLAZE

MAKES A SCANT ½ CUP (100 ML)

1 tbsp. silken soft tofu
½ tsp. soy sauce
1 tsp. white miso
Pinch freshly ground black pepper
2 egg yolks, beaten

In a blender, mix the tofu, soy sauce, miso and pepper. Blend in the egg yolks at low speed.

TORO AGUA DE CHILE

*A*gua de chile is a Mexican dipping sauce made of puréed red jalapeños, cilantro, salt and water. When I tasted this wonderful sauce with seafood in Mexico, I immediately thought the freshness, spice and acidity fairly embodied the Nobu style. So I dreamed up this rich tuna belly paired with a soft jelly of *agua de chile* for surprising texture. Cubes of avocado help tone down the heat, and that drop or two of soy sauce was Nobu's idea. Thank you, Nobu! —*T.B.*

Agua de Chile Jelly (makes 1⅛ cups/270 ml)
2 to 3 red jalapeños
1 small ripe tomato
1 tsp. chopped cilantro
Pinch chopped garlic
1 cup (240 ml) spring water
Juice of 1 lime
¼ tsp. rice vinegar
Pinch salt
1½ sheets gelatin (2.3 g), soaked in water

Additional Ingredients
About 3 cups crushed ice
½ avocado
Juice of ½ lime
Salt
12 pieces *o-toro* fatty tuna, each 1½ in. (4 cm) square, 3 oz. (90 g) total
4 tbsp. *tamari* soy sauce
6 large cilantro leaves, torn in half

1. Make the "Agua de Chile" Jelly: Remove the seeds from one of the jalapeños, leaving the others intact. Purée them in a blender with the other ingredients, except the gelatin, and pass through a strainer into a saucepan. Place the pan over low heat and warm the mixture until tepid. Squeeze the gelatin sheets to drain and add into the mixture. Stir to fully dissolve. Transfer to a container and refrigerate until set to a loose jelly consistency.

2. Divide the jelly into 12 serving bowls and place over crushed ice.

3. Dice the avocado and mix with the lime juice and salt.

4. Place the toro over the jelly and pour about 1 tsp. tamari on the side. Garnish with the avocado and cilantro.

PLANTAIN CHIPS WITH OCOPA SAUCE AND PONZU MAYO

South Americans eat plantains in many ways, depending on the country and region—*mofongo*, *yo-yo*, *tostones*—they're easily as versatile as potatoes. Plantain dishes are often plain, but here we pair them with Nobu's Ponzu Mayo and Ocopa Sauce, made with a Peruvian black mint called *huacatay*.

—*T.B.*

2 plantains
Vegetable oil for deep-frying
Salt
4 tbsp. Ocopa Sauce (recipe follows)
4 tbsp. Ponzu Mayo (recipe follows)

Trim the ends of the plantains, peel, and slice lengthwise on a mandoline. Deep-fry in 280 °F (140 °C) oil until golden and crisp. Drain on a paper-lined dish and season with salt while hot. Serve with the sauces.

OCOPA SAUCE

MAKES 1½ CUPS (360 ML)

3 tbsp. *ají amarillo* paste
½ block silken tofu, 5 oz. (150 g)
1 tbsp. soy milk (or more)
¼ cup (60 ml) olive oil
½ white onion, finely chopped
2 cloves garlic, finely chopped
1 tbsp. chopped *huacatay* black mint
1 tbsp. unsalted peanuts, toasted and chopped
2 tsp. soy sauce
Salt and pepper

1. Purée the ají amarillo paste, tofu and soy milk to a smooth paste in a blender. Set aside.

2. Place the olive oil, onion and garlic in a frying pan over low heat and cook slowly until the onion becomes soft and slightly transparent. Add the huacatay and peanuts and cook for 1 minute. Mix to a smooth paste in a blender.

3. Combine the two pastes and season to taste with soy sauce, salt and pepper. Add a little more soy milk to thin if necessary.

PONZU MAYO

MAKES SCANT ⅔ CUP (150 ML)

Ponzu
1 tbsp. soy sauce
2 tbsp. rice vinegar
½ tbsp. lemon juice
1 piece dried *kombu*, ½ in. (1 cm) square

7 tbsp. mayonnaise

1. First make the Ponzu: Combine all Ponzu ingredients and refrigerate overnight (at least 8 hours).

2. Combine the Ponzu with the mayonnaise.

AVOCADO WEDGES WITH TUNA AND MISO

"You mean this isn't prosciutto with melon?" You'll surprise all the party guests with this one. *Akami* tuna and avocado are such a perfect combination; each makes the other taste even better. Add to that the special fermented flavor of miso and sour lemon. Red tuna meat is low in saturated fat and leaves a clean aftertaste: perfect with a chilled sparkling wine—or sake, of course.

—*N.M.*

Avocado Salsa
2 avocados
Juice of 2 lemons
Salt to taste

4 avocados
4 oz. (120 g) *akami* tuna loin (bigeye or bluefin if possible)
Sea salt
4 tbsp. yellow miso

1. Make the Avocado Salsa: Purée the all ingredients in a blender until smooth. Set aside.

2. Peel and cut the 4 avocados in half, remove the pits and cut each half into 4 wedges.

3. Trim the tuna, remove any sinew and cut into thin strips.

4. Place the tuna over the avocado wedges and season with sea salt. Place a spoonful of avocado sauce with a little miso on top next to each piece.

BRAISED CRISPY OCTOPUS IN EDAMAME PURÉE

With a touch of Japanese herbs, this crisp-braised octopus, redolent of soy sauce, would make a brilliant snack along with sake, but puréed *edamame* instantly transforms it into full-fledged restaurant fare. Adding *dashi* to the purée would give it more *umami*, though here we've blended in a hint of butter for richness—the choice is yours. We then accent it with a dot of *kanzuri* Japanese chili paste, which is made by laying salted red peppers on snow, then adding *yuzu*, rice and salt and letting it ferment for three years. It adds that special complex kick. —*T.B.*

SERVES 6

Marinated Octopus
2 cups (480 ml) Dashi Stock (p. 183)
1 tbsp. *tamari* soy sauce
1 slice ginger
Pinch freshly ground black pepper
Pinch *shichimi* spice powder
6 baby octopus
Pinch chopped fresh red chili pepper
1 tbsp. extra-virgin olive oil

Edamame Purée
1 cup (260 g) shelled fresh *edamame*
1 cup (240 ml) Dashi Stock (p. 183)
¼ cup (60 g) butter
Salt and freshly ground white pepper

1 tsp. *kanzuri* fermented chili paste, store-bought

1. Make the Marinated Octopus: In a saucepan, bring the dashi, tamari, ginger, black pepper, and shichimi to a boil. Plunge in the octopus for 20 seconds to cook. Remove the pan from heat and take out the octopus. Allow the marinade to cool to room temperature, then return the octopus to the pan. Stir in the red chili pepper and olive oil. Marinate for 30 minutes.

2. Make the Edamame Purée: Heat the edamame in the dashi stock. Strain the edamame out of the dashi (reserve the dashi) and place in a blender while hot. Purée the edamame, adding the dashi little by little to control the consistency. Add the butter and season with salt and white pepper. The purée should have a somewhat loose consistency. Keep warm.

3. Remove the octopus from the marinade. Grill until crisp. Bring the marinade to a gentle simmer and reduce to a syrup.

4. Divide the edamame purée into serving cups and put in the octopus, tentacle-side up. Spoon a little marinade reduction over. Dot with the kanzuri.

PATTY PAN SQUASH WITH SPICY VEGETABLES

One ingredient we use a lot for finger food is the disc-shaped summer squash known locally as "patty pan squash" or "scallop squash." They can be scooped out to form edible cups, so you don't need plates or forks. These squash retain a lot of moisture—one bite will fill your mouth with marvelous soupy goodness. We hardly see them in Japan, but they're readily available at organic markets in America and Europe during the summer months, so please give them a try. Despite its Western look, this dish skillfully combines miso and *tobanjan* chili paste for a marriage of fresh Asian flavors—very Nobu. —*N.M.*

MAKES 32 PIECES

32 small patty pan squash
2 small red peppers, diced fine
2 small yellow bell peppers, diced fine
1 red onion, diced fine
2 zucchinis, green outside only, diced fine
4 to 6 tbsp. Spicy Shallot Pepper Miso (recipe follows)

1. Cut off the tops of the squash and scoop out the insides with a melon baller. Steam gently until cooked al dente (you can also place in simmering water for about 4 minutes). Place in ice water to halt the cooking.

2. Mix the diced vegetables with the Spicy Shallot Pepper Miso and stuff into the squash. Place the lids on top. If not serving immediately, warm gently in a low oven just before serving to enhance the flavors.

SPICY SHALLOT PEPPER MISO
MAKES ABOUT ¾ CUP (180 ML)

6 shallots, finely diced
2 cloves garlic, finely diced
2 tsp. cubeb peppercorns, toasted and ground
3 tbsp. Sake Soy (p. 16)
2½ tbsp. Den Miso (p. 156)
1 tsp. *tobanjan* chili paste
Juice of 3 limes

Combine all ingredients.

SAKE-STEAMED ABALONE CHALACA

Chalaca salsa—originally from Callao, Lima's port district—is made from tomato, onion, Peruvian corn and *ají limo* chile. Typically served on mussels, the sour acidity and spicy heat lends itself to almost any seafood. For a Nobu twist, we add *yuzu* and serve our chalaca with sake-steamed baby abalone. Just remember, baby abalone are very tender, so don't heat them for very long or they'll shrink. —*T.B.*

MAKES 10 PIECES

10 fresh baby abalone
1 cup (240 ml) sake
1 cup (240 ml) Dashi Stock (p. 183)
1 piece *kombu*, 2 in. (5 cm) square
10 tsp. Chalaca Style Salsa (recipe follows)
5 cilantro leaves, torn in half

1. Clean the abalone and their shells. Reserve the shells and set aside. Place the abalone, sake, dashi and kombu in a pot and bring to a boil. Simmer gently for 30 to 40 minutes. Allow to cool in the liquid.

2. Serve each abalone in its shell with a teaspoonful of the Chalaca Style Salsa. Garnish with the cilantro leaves.

CHALACA STYLE SALSA   MAKES ABOUT ⅔ CUP (160 ML)

½ medium tomato, skin and seeds removed, cut into ⅛ in. (3 mm) dice
¼ small red onion
Pinch chopped *ají limo*
Pinch chopped garlic
3 tbsp. steamed Peruvian corn kernels
Juice of 2 limes

1½ tbsp. extra-virgin olive oil
1 tsp. *yuzu* juice
1½ tsp. salt
½ tsp. freshly ground white pepper
½ tbsp. chopped cilantro

Mix all ingredients except salt, pepper and cilantro. Season with salt and pepper to taste. Cilantro should be added just before serving to retain color.

CONCH TIRADITO, NOBU STYLE

Tough and chewy raw conch meat becomes quite palatable when sliced ultra-thin with a well-honed sashimi knife. My *tiraditos* always change, incorporating a variety of different local seasonal ingredients, but the presentation maintains a basically Japanese aesthetic: foods are arranged on the plate artistically, with sincerity and *kokoro*. Here we use a Himalayan pink salt block for our canvas and lay down thin "brushstrokes" of cucumber, then sprinkle flakes of Himalayan black salt over conch slices . . . and behold, a tiradito worthy of a painting! —*N.M.*

Single Malt and Lucuma (see p. 189 for recipe)

A chilled Himalayan pink salt block makes a perfect underlay for sashimi, letting just the right hint of saltiness slowly pass up and naturally cure the fish. Conversely, you can roast the salt sizzling hot, then lay it over the *tiradito* ingredients to sear them right before your guests' eyes, much like *toban yaki* cookery. Either way, this salt block directly confirms my conviction that cold dishes should be served cold and hot dishes piping hot. Also, varying your serving dishes can really add to the fun of party food.

—*N.M.*

Single Malt and Lucuma (see p. 189 for recipe)

MAKES 18 THIN SLICES

About 1⅓ oz. (40 g) fresh conch

18 cilantro leaves

1 tsp. Ají Rocoto Vidrio (p. 25)

2 tbsp. *yuzu* juice

½ tsp. Himalayan black salt

1 Japanese cucumber, thinly sliced lengthwise (optional)

1. Using the heel of a knife or mallet, pound the conch flesh on both sides to tenderize. Cut into 18 paper-thin slices.

2. If using, lay the cucumber slices on a platter. Arrange the conch slices on top. Place a cilantro leaf on each, and dot the Ají Rocoto Vidrio on the cilantro. Sprinkle with yuzu juice and Himalayan black salt.

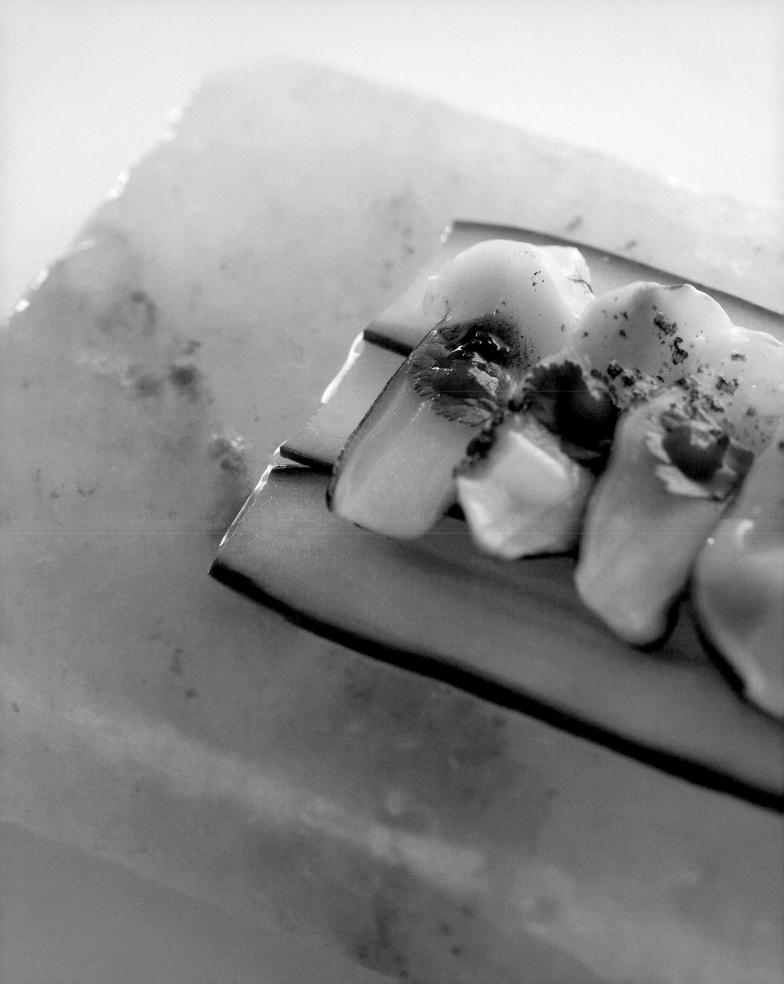

TORO "PASTRAMI"

Smoking foods to create new flavors is a truly American culinary aesthetic. For this dish, we smoke *toro* tuna belly for fifteen minutes, bringing out that special tuna fat richness. Thick slices can be delicious, but here we firm the tuna up a little in the freezer, then slice it paper thin with a sashimi knife. The way the fat just melts on your tongue—heavenly! For garnishes, rather than crisp leaf vegetables, we choose tender mandoline-slivered white and green asparagus. Toss everything together for the ultimate airy, delicate salad. —*N.M.*

MAKES 18 SMALL DISHES

1 lb. (450 g) *chu-toro* tuna belly

1 tbsp. Pastrami Spice Mix (recipe follows)

1 cup cherry wood chips

1 tbsp. dry rice

6 spears jumbo green asparagus, blanched

6 spears white asparagus, blanched

Pinch salt

2 tbsp. Yuzu Ponzu (p. 183)

18 Garlic Chips (p. 183)

18 slices lemon grass, deep-fried

1. Coat the chu-toro with the Pastrami Spice Mix. Prepare a cold smoking setup with a pan, a smaller perforated pan or rack that fits inside, and a lid. Cover any gaps with aluminum foil.

2. Heat the cherry wood and rice in a separate dry pan until smoking, then place in the bottom pan of the cold smoking setup. Set the perforated pan or rack inside, place the toro on the rack, and cover. Leave for 15 minutes.

3. Place the toro in the freezer for 1 hour to make it easier to slice thinly. (A professional meat slicer is ideal, but a very sharp knife will do.) Slice the green and white asparagus lengthwise on a mandoline. Dress with the Yuzu Ponzu.

4. Drape the toro slices over the asparagus. Divide into serving plates and sprinkle with salt. Garnish with the fried lemon grass and Garlic Chips.

PASTRAMI SPICE MIX

MAKES ABOUT 2½ TBSP.

2 tsp. black peppercorns

1 tsp. white peppercorns

1 tsp. coriander seeds

1 tsp. yellow mustard seeds

1 large clove garlic, minced

1 tbsp. salt

1½ tsp. brown sugar

2 tsp. smoked paprika powder

In a mortar or spice grinder, grind the peppercorns, coriander and mustard seeds into a semi-fine powder. Mix in the rest of the ingredients.

NEW STYLE FLOUNDER

The Nobu standard New Style Sashimi takes on a new look. Usually we arrange sashimi flat on a plate, though rolling can make the pieces easier to eat at parties; often we secure the rolls with toothpicks, or as in the photo, let guests pick them up with chopsticks or bamboo skewers. While here we've rolled fresh-caught local flounder in chives with very thin shavings of wild *udo* shoots and ginger, I recommend using the very best sashimi-grade fish you can find where you live. Shellfish or even beef can also be delicious this way. Make sure to use chives and ginger, because these go well with fish, but if you can't find udo, thinly sliced daikon radish or carrot will do. A hot drizzle of "new style oil" will cook the fish just enough to please even non-sashimi-eaters. —*N.M.*

MAKES 12 PIECES

6 oz. (170 g) flounder fillet, skinned
½ cup (30 g) chives, cut into 2 in. (5 cm) lengths
4 garlic cloves, puréed
½ thumb-size knob ginger, julienned
2 in. (5 cm) long *udo* stalk, julienned
1 tbsp. Yuzu Soy (p. 121)

3 tbsp. pure olive oil
1 tsp. sesame oil

12 *kinome* leaves
1 tsp. sesame seeds, toasted

1. Lay the fillet at an angle on the cutting board. Using a *yanagi* knife (or a very sharp slicer), slice 12 thin pieces by pressing your offhand fingertips against the fillet and drawing the knife through the fillet from heel to tip.

2. Dot the slices with a little garlic and wrap each around a bundle of udo, ginger and chives. Line up the rolls on a heatproof platter or tray and dress with Yuzu Soy.

3. Combine the oils, heat until smoking and pour over the rolls.

4. Transfer the rolls with their sauce to a serving plate. Garnish with the kinome leaves and sesame seeds.

CAUSA CROQUETTES WITH AJÍ AMARILLO AIOLI

Peru is said to have 4,000 kinds of pota-toes. Among these the most popular vari-ety is the *papa amarilla* or Peruvian yellow potato—the best for mashing—which is tra-ditionally mixed with Peruvian lemon, onion, oil and red chile to make *causa*. To turn this very humble home-cooked dish into party food, we shape the causa mash into little balls and bread them with egg, flour and *panko* to make bite-size croquettes. For a dipping sauce we use yellow *ají amarillo* chilis, which are extremely spicy but also very fruity as only Peruvian chilis can be. Peru has a wealth of ingredients to excite and inspire chefs the world over. —*T.B.*

MAKES 12 CROQUETTES

Causa Base

1 lb. (45 kg) Peruvian yellow potatoes
1 tbsp. Ají Amarillo Purée (recipe follows)
1 tsp. salt
1¼ tsp. freshly ground black pepper
Juice of 2 limes

¼ red onion, sliced thin
Juice of 1 lime
½ tsp. salt
1 egg, beaten
2 tbsp. all-purpose flour
3 tbsp. *panko*, ground finely in a food processor
½ cup (120 ml) Ají Amarillo Aioli (recipe follows)
10 micro cilantro sprouts
Vegetable oil for deep-frying

1. First make the Causa Base: Steam the yellow potatoes and pass through a ricer. Mix with the ají amarillo pureé, salt, pepper and lime juice.

2. Marinate the sliced red onions in the salt and lime juice.

3. Divide the Causa Base into 12 pieces and form into balls. Dust with flour and dip in egg, then panko. Deep-fry at 340 °F (170 °C) until golden brown.

4. Place a pool of aioli in a small dish and top with a croquette. Garnish with the mari-nated onions.

AJÍ AMARILLO AIOLI
MAKES ½ CUP (120 ML)

6 tbsp. mayonnaise
3 tbsp. Ají Amarillo Purée (recipe follows)

Combine both ingredients.

AJÍ AMARILLO PURÉE
MAKES 1½ CUPS (360 ML)

8 oz. (240 g) *ají amarillo*, fresh or frozen, trimmed
2 tbsp. rice vinegar
4 tbsp. sugar
1 tbsp. olive oil

Place all ingredients in a blender except the oil. Mix to a purée. Add the oil little by little while blending at low speed to form an emulsion.

FLORIDA DEEP FRIES

Groups of ten or more often reserve tables at Nobu Miami, so it can be like hosting several small parties simultaneously throughout the restaurant. Here's a treat we often get asked to make for those special occasions. Visitors to Miami really go for deep-fried Biscayne Bay shrimp (pink shrimp), scallops and stone crab claws—all authentic regional tastes. The shrimp we deep-fry *kara-age* style, dusting them with corn starch instead of using egg. We prepare the other two items as tempura, coating them thoroughly with a flour, egg and water batter. When people see this eye-catching party platter served at the next table they invariably say, "We'll have that too!" —*T.B.*

CRISPY BISCAYNE BAY SHRIMP

SERVES 4

32 to 40 live bay shrimp
1 cup (240 ml) sake
1 cup (160 g) potato starch
1 tbsp. salt (more for soaking shrimp)
2 tsp. *shichimi* spice powder
1 lemon, cut into wedges
2 cups (480 ml) peanut oil for frying

1. Soak the shrimp in salted water for 20 minutes to clean, then toss with the sake and pat dry.

2. Dredge the shrimp in the potato starch and deep-fry in the 360 °F (180 °C) oil until crispy, about 40 seconds. Shake off excess oil and toss with salt and shichimi.

3. Serve in a Japanese paper cone with a lemon wedge on the side.

SCALLOP TEMPURA

MAKES 10 PIECES

Yuzu Truffle Teriyaki Sauce
1 cup (240 ml) chicken stock
4 tbsp. sugar
3 tbsp. soy sauce
2 tsp. *kudzu* starch, dissolved in 3 tsp. water
1 tbsp. chopped black truffle
1 tsp. *yuzu* juice

10 scallops, live if possible
40 slices black truffle
Salt and pepper
1 tsp. truffle oil
10 napa cabbage leaves, blanched
2 tbsp. all-purpose flour
1 recipe Tempura Batter (p. 183)
½ tsp. sea salt
Vegetable oil for deep-frying

1. First make Yuzu Truffle Teriyaki Sauce: In a saucepan, combine the chicken stock, sugar and soy sauce and bring to a gentle simmer. Cook for 2 minutes and add the dissolved kudzu to thicken. Remove from heat and add the truffle and yuzu juice. Set aside.

2. Slice each scallop horizontally into 5 thin rounds and lay out on a surface. Season with salt, pepper, and truffle oil. Place a truffle slice on 4 of every 5 scallop slices and restack the scallops so that 4 truffle slices are sandwiched alternately between 5 scallop slices. You should have 10 pieces. Bundle each piece tightly in a napa cabbage leaf. Refrigerate for 1-2 hours.

3. Heat the oil to 360 °F (180 °C). Mix the Tempura Batter ingredients.

4. Dredge each bundle in the flour and dip in the batter, shaking off any excess. Deep-fry about 1 minute, until the batter becomes crisp. The scallops should be a little underdone.

5. Trim the ends and cut in half. While hot, sprinkle with a little sea salt. Serve with the Yuzu Truffle Teriyaki Sauce in dipping cups.

STONE CRAB CLAW TEMPURA WITH KEY LIME PONZU

Key Lime Ponzu Sauce
½ cup (120 ml) rice vinegar
¼ cup (60 ml) soy sauce
1 tsp. lemon juice
1 tsp. key lime juice

10 medium stone crab claws
½ cup (70 g) flour
1 recipe Tempura Batter (p. 183)
Vegetable oil for frying

Garnish
1 key lime, thinly sliced

1. Make the Key Lime Ponzu Sauce: Combine all ingredients and set aside.

2. Crack the crab claws and remove all of the shell except the "thumb." Preheat the oil to 360 °F (180 °C).

3. Holding the claw by its "thumb," dip in the flour, then batter. Deep-fry until the batter colors but the claw is still underdone, about 50 seconds.

4. Serve with the Key Lime Ponzu Sauce in a dipping cups. Garnish with the key lime slices.

FOIE CROQUETTE WITH YUZU MARMALADE AND KIWICHA

Strange as it might seem, croquettes filled with creamy béchamel sauce are standard fare in Japan. Best eaten piping hot, the gooey interior is supposed to spread nicely in your mouth. The same goes for this Foie Croquette. The gelatin mixture oozes with *foie gras* richness when eaten hot from the fryer. Because the filling is very soft, we wanted a contrasting texture for the crust and substituted *kiwicha* for *panko* breadcrumbs. Also called amaranth, *kiwicha* grain was a major staple of the pre-Columbian Andes, and was even used in ceremonies. The fine-textured crunch is something else! —*T.B.*

1 whole *foie gras*, 1¾ lb. (780 g), cleaned and cut into pieces

1 tbsp. plum wine

1 tbsp. brandy

1 tbsp. sake

2 tsp. Peruvian pink salt or any coarse salt

1 tsp. freshly ground black pepper

5 sheets (7.5 g) gelatin, soaked in cold water

Breading

1 cup (45 g) *panko*, ground fine in a food processor

1 cup (150 g) *kiwicha*

1 cup (125 g) all-purpose flour

1 egg, beaten

Vegetable oil for sautéing and deep-frying

Yuzu Jam (recipe follows)

Micro amaranth, as garnish

Kumquat slices, as garnish

1. Sauté the foie gras briefly, then flambé with the mixture of plum wine, brandy and sake. Place in a blender with the pink salt and pepper. Squeeze the gelatin to drain and add to the blender. Mix to a smooth paste. Pass through a fine sieve to remove any veins or other debris from the foie gras.

2. Pour into a tray large enough so that the mixture comes to ½ in. (1 cm) depth. Refrigerate until set.

3. Cut the jellied foie gras into ½ in. (1 cm) cubes. Combine the panko and kiwicha in a bowl. Dust the cubes in flour, then dip in the beaten egg, then in the panko and kiwicha mixture. Deep-fry at 340 °F (170 °C).

4. Place a little Yuzu Jam on a spoon and top with a croquette. Garnish with micro amaranth and a kumquat slice.

YUZU JAM

MAKES ABOUT 3 CUPS (720 ML)

1 cup (100 g) *yuzu* peel, bitter pith removed

2 cups (190 g) granulated sugar

3 tbsp. (40 ml) *mirin*

3 tbsp. (40 ml) yuzu juice

⅓ cup (80 ml) orange juice

1 tsp. pectin

Place the yuzu peel, sugar, mirin, orange juice, and yuzu juice in a non-reactive pot. Bring to a rapid boil for 5 to 10 minutes. Remove from heat. Add the pectin, then return the pot to medium high heat and cook for 3 minutes, stirring constantly. Cool to room temperature.

SEARED STRIPED BASS WITH BLACK BEANS AND RICE

A little twist on the classic Cuban dish *moros con cristianos*. The cooked rice is mixed with sake, a little black bean paste and fermented black beans. The fish is finished with ginger and chives and seared with hot sesame oil. The flavoring leans toward Cuban-Chinese, so we serve it with chopsticks and *renge* spoons to complete the mood. Besides striped bass, pompano, scallops or shrimp also do very nicely this way. —T.B.

MAKES 12 PIECES

10 oz. (280 g) striped bass fillet, skin-on

Salt and freshly ground black pepper

1 tsp. fermented black bean paste (*dou chi jiang*)

3 tbsp. sake

2 tsp. whole fermented black beans (*dou chi*)

½ cup (90 g) Cooked Rice (p. 184)

1 tbsp. olive oil

1 thumb-size knob ginger, grated, juice squeezed and reserved

2 tsp. chopped chives

1 tsp. ginger julienne

2 tbsp. sesame oil

Salt and pepper

1. Cut the fillet into twelve 1½ in. (4 cm) strips and season with salt and pepper.

2. Mix the black bean paste with sake and whole beans in a heat-proof cup. Cover, place in a steamer, and steam for 5 minutes. Add the cooked rice and steam for 2 more minutes. Set aside.

3. Heat the olive oil and sear the fish over medium heat until the skin is crisp. Turn the fish over and remove from heat, but leave in the pan to finish cooking. Heat the sesame oil to smoking hot in another saucepan. Sprinkle the ginger juice and chives on top of the fish and pour the hot sesame oil over to sear.

4. Place about a teaspoon of the rice on each serving spoon. Arrange the beans, fish pieces, ginger julienne and chives on top.

BRANZINO WITH FLORIDA AMAZU SAUCE

This is branzino tempura; however, we substitute vodka for half the water in the batter. In Japan, it's not uncommon to use *shochu* spirits in tempura batter. The alcohol makes the tempura fry up extra light and crisp. Another trick for crispy tempura is not to whisk the batter too much, because over-blending causes the gluten in the flour to develop, making the tempura heavy and chewy when fried. It's fine for the batter to have a few small lumps. We use Florida-grown Minneola oranges for our *amazu* dipping sauce. They're honey-sweet and have a bright flowery fragrance. —*N.M.*

1 whole branzino, about 1⅓ lb. (580 g), scaled,
  filleted and boned (carcass reserved for presentation)

2 to 3 tbsp. all-purpose flour

1 cup (240 ml) Vodka Tempura Batter
  (p. 183, substitute vodka for the water)

Vegetable oil for frying

1 serrano chili pepper, sliced fine

½ red onion, thinly sliced and placed in ice water

¼ cup (5 g) loosely packed cilantro, chopped
  and whole leaves

½ cup (7 g) micro cilantro

2 to 3 tbsp. Florida Amazu Sauce (recipe follows)

Daikon radish shreds, for presentation

1. Cut the branzino into pieces small enough to be eaten in about two bites (about 10 pieces). Lightly dredge the fish in flour and dip into the Vodka Tempura Batter. Deep-fry at 360 °F (180 °C) until lightly colored. Transfer to a paper-lined dish to drain any excess oil. Dredge the carcass, if using, in flour and deep-fry until crisp and lightly browned.

2. Pile the fried fish on a plate and garnish with onion, a few slices of serrano chili pepper, chopped cilantro and micro cilantro. Spoon some of the Florida Amazu Sauce over, or serve the sauce in a dipping cup. Place the daikon radish shreds and fried carcass on the side.

FLORIDA AMAZU SAUCE

1 tbsp. rice vinegar

3 tbsp. granulated sugar

1 tsp. salt

1 small piece *kombu*, ½ in. (1 cm) square

3 tbsp. (40 ml) Minneola orange juice

Place the rice vinegar, granulated sugar, salt and kombu in a small saucepan over low heat and dissolve the sugar and salt. Cool and remove the kombu. Add the orange juice and set aside.

ROASTED BROCCOLI AND CAULIFLOWER WITH RED AND GREEN JALAPEÑO SALSA

This salsa-based dish will work with almost any vegetable. Just make sure to loosen up the florets so the liquid can coat them thoroughly. Here we oven-roast rather than boiling or steaming, lightly browning the tips of the vegetables for a nice, hearty fragrance. Never discard the thick broccoli stems; just peel away the tough outer layer of skin and leave all that meaty texture. It's precious—you only get a little per stalk. —*N.M.*

MAKES 20 PIECES

1 to 2 heads broccoli
1 head cauliflower
Salt and freshly ground black pepper
Olive oil
1 cup (240 ml) Dashi Stock (p. 183)

Red Jalapeño Salsa (makes 1 cup /240 ml)
2 tsp. chopped jalapeño
½ white onion, finely chopped
1 medium tomato, chopped
1⅓ tbsp. extra-virgin olive oil
¼ cup (60 ml) lemon juice
⅔ tsp. salt

Green Jalapeño Salsa (makes scant 1 cup /200 ml)
2 tsp. chopped jalapeño
1 white onion, finely chopped
1⅓ tbsp. extra-virgin olive oil
¼ cup (60 ml) lemon juice
⅔ tsp. salt

1. Make the Red Jalapeño Salsa and Green Jalapeño Salsa by combining the ingredients for each in separate bowls. Set aside.

2. Trim the broccoli stems into cylinders, then slice. Divide the broccoli and cauliflower into florets. Blanch the florets in boiling salted water and shock in ice water. Drain. Cook the broccoli stems in boiling salted water and shock in ice water. Drain.

3. Heat the oven to 480 °F (250 °C). Season the florets with salt and pepper, then coat with the olive oil. Roast until the tips are slightly browned.

4. Place the dashi stock in a saucepan over low heat and season with salt and pepper to taste. When the stock is warm, add the broccoli stems, poach for a few seconds, then remove from heat and cool in the liquid to room temperature.

5. Arrange the broccoli stem slices in 20 small dishes. In half the dishes, spoon the Red Jalapeño Salsa over and top with a broccoli floret. For the other half, spoon the Green Jalapeño Salsa over and top with a cauliflower floret. Alternate the dishes to display.

NOBU FISH AND CHIPS

any customers order Fish and Chips at Nobu, maybe because we always add a special twist. Like mixing salt and green tea powder, or salt and curry powder, each a standard in its own right. If you have time, try skinning, seeding and slow-drying familiar vegetables, then grinding them into powders. Here I've used tomato powder, but beet or carrot powder would also add color. I like to use Maldon salt from near my hometown, but use your own favorite and make it special for you.

—T.B.

SERVES 6 TO 8

3 sweet potatoes
Vegetable oil for deep-frying

1 lb. (450 g) black cod (grouper or bass work well too), cleaned
2 to 3 tbsp. all-purpose flour
6 cups (1.4 L) Beer Tempura Batter
    (p. 183, substitute beer for the water)
Vegetable oil for deep-frying
Salt and freshly ground black pepper

1 *yuzu*, cut in half
Tomato, Curry and Green Tea Salts (recipe follows)

1. Peel the sweet potatoes and cut into 4 in. (10 cm)-long batons. Deep-fry at 280 °F (140 °C) until soft, about 5 minutes. They should be pale but cooked through. Drain on a paper towel. Allow to rest and cool at least 30 minutes as this will make crisper chips.

2. Cut the fish into 3 in. (7.5 cm)-long batons and dust in flour. Dip in the Beer Tempura Batter and deep-fry at 360 °F (180 °C). Re-fry the sweet potato at the same temperature until crisp. Lightly sprinkle with salt and pepper while hot.

3. Serve the sweet potato in a paper cone and place the fish on the side. Make little mounds of the three salts and arrange yuzu halves alongside.

TOMATO, CURRY AND GREEN TEA SALTS

Tomato skin and seeds	Dry the skin and seeds of a tomato overnight in an oven at the lowest possible temperature. Grind into powder. Mix 1 part tomato powder with 1 part salt. Mix 1 part green tea powder with 1.5 parts salt and lightly grind together to make green tea salt. Do the same with the curry powder to make curry salt.
Curry powder	
Green tea powder	
Good-quality salt	

LUNCHEONS

■■■■■■■■■■

BABY RADISHES WITH TOMATILLO SALSA

A vegetable dish topped with a vegetable salsa—what more healthy way to kick off a lunch party? Radishes, like heirloom tomatoes, come in all different varieties and colors. Specialty produce is hard to find at big supermarkets, but if you're lucky enough to live near a good local grocer or farmers' market, please support them with your business. Fresh local produce can be delicious just plain, sliced thin or lightly blanched. And if you tire of olive oil, salt and pepper, try experimenting with vegetable salsas; they're a good way to enjoy eating more vegetables. The Miami crowd really goes for salads—almost as much as cocktails! —*LB*

Tomatillo Salsa

4 medium tomatillos, cut into ¼ in. (6 mm) dice

¼ serrano chili pepper, finely chopped

¼ clove garlic

1 tsp. chopped cilantro leaves

1 tbsp. chopped white onion

Pinch ground cumin seeds

Pinch salt

2 tsp. Tosazu (recipe below)

Juice of 1 lime

5 each of at least three different types of baby radish, such as Chinese, watermelon or greentop

Sea salt

1. Make the Tomatillo Salsa: Combine all ingredients and set aside.

2. Peel the radishes and trim into even cylinders. Slice as thinly as possible into regular disks on a mandoline. Soak in ice water until crisp. Drain well.

3. Arrange the radish slices on a plate in concentric rings by color, starting from the edge of the plate. Make sure that each disk overlaps the previous one. Sprinkle with the Tomatillo Salsa and sea salt.

TOSAZU

MAKES ⅓ CUP (80 ML)

3 tbsp. soy sauce

4 tbsp. rice vinegar

3 tbsp. (2 g) dried bonito flakes

Heat the soy sauce and rice vinegar in a small saucepan until the mixture begins to steam. Remove from heat and add the bonito flakes. Cool to room temperature and strain.

Nobu Restaurants make a point of hospitality and *kokoro*: easy to say, but very difficult to do well. In order to put your *kokoro* into everything, you have to be healthy in your *kokoro*.

As a chef, I want to go to different countries and meet people and absorb all kinds of influences, like Nobu has. A chef has to have many facets; it's not enough just to prepare food. You have to know your ingredients, and understand stock management, restaurant operations, how to communicate with staff—things you don't learn by going home after a long day in the kitchen and studying recipes. I try to be open, to learn from everyone and everything. I do my share of teaching in the kitchen, but a good teacher should also be a good student.

When I first became a cook in my teens, I was always in a hurry. I pushed myself to learn all the rules of traditional English cookery and classic French cuisine. I can say it now, but it took a good ten years to get to where I could call myself a chef. You can't rush it. —*T.B.*

RACK OF LAMB WITH SHISO PANKO CRUST

It's nice to see your host slice and serve meat right there before you, saying, "Wait till you taste this Colorado lamb, it's the best in all of America." This kind of very personal, very communal touch really showcases the food and heightens anticipation among the guests. Rack of Lamb is a party standard, but of course we've given it a few Nobu twists. First, there are the *kampyo* dried gourd strips wound around the rib bones—please read the notes on this page for more detail. Then, there's the *panko* crust. We partially roast the lamb, let it cool slightly, then slather on mustard and roll it in panko breadcrumbs before returning it to the oven to roast until golden crisp. The herb *shiso*, mixed in with the breadcrumbs, adds a uniquely Japanese note to the flavor of the meat. —*N.M.*

No matter how consummately French you go when serving lamb, I'm sure you don't want the bare bones showing. Since capping the rib tips with aluminum foil is hardly elegant, we instead wrap them in *kampyo*—thin strips planed from *fukube* gourds in long spirals and sold dry. Our sushi bar simmers them in soy sauce and sugar for kampyo rolls, but here they're left plain and white like in the photo. See how lovely they look wrapped around the bones like fancy ribbons. —*N.M.*

MAKES 6 CHOPS

1 rack (6 bones) lamb, frenched
Handful *kampyo* (dried gourd strips)
2 tsp. clarified butter
1 tbsp. mustard powder, mixed with 1 tbsp. warm water
1 tsp. Nobu-style Saikyo Miso (p. 42)
½ cup (120 ml) *panko*
¼ cup (60 ml) chopped *shiso* leaves
Salt and pepper

1. Wrap the exposed bones of the lamb with the kampyo.

2. Season the lamb with salt and pepper. Heat the clarified butter in a frying pan and sear the lamb.

3. Place the rack into a 400 °F (200 °C) oven and cook for 8 minutes, turning once. Remove from the oven and let rest for 5 minutes. (Leave the oven on.)

4. Mix the mustard with the Nobu-style Saikyo Miso in a bowl. Mix the panko with shiso leaves in a separate bowl. Spread the miso mixture over the rack, and roll in the shiso-panko mixture.

5. Return the rack to in the oven for 5 minutes until the crust browns slightly. Transfer to a warm plate to rest for 2 minutes. Carve into 6 chops and serve.

FLOUNDER SASHIMI SALAD WITH YUZU HONEY AJÍ LIMO DRESSING

Some Americans have difficulty eating raw fish. We dreamed up sashimi salads like this in order to turn them on to how good fresh sashimi can be! This dish exemplifies the versatility of Nobu cuisine in transforming dishes. By now sashimi salads are everywhere, but this dressing is something special: sweet, sour and spicy, it goes well with virtually any fish, white-fleshed or not—even crab and other crustaceans. Needless to say, you can substitute other citrus for the *yuzu* or your favorite chili for the *ají limo*. Serve this on a large platter for the full effect at parties! —*N.M.*

MAKES 10 PORTIONS

1 whole medium flounder, 8 oz. (240 g) total, filleted and skinned

¼ tsp. salt

2 tbsp. Yuzu Honey Ají Limo Dressing (recipe follows)

2 tsp. extra-virgin olive oil

1 small red bell pepper, thinly sliced

1 small yellow bell pepper, thinly sliced

1 small red onion, thinly sliced

Handful mixed micro greens

1. Cut the fish into paper-thin slices and lay onto a large round platter. Sprinkle with salt.

2. Spoon the Yuzu Honey Ají Limo dressing over the fish. Finish with olive oil.

3. Scatter the sliced vegetables over the fish. Lay the micro greens on top, leaves facing up as they are in the package.

YUZU HONEY AJÍ LIMO DRESSING
MAKES 1 CUP (240 ML)

1 cup (240 ml) *yuzu* juice

1 fresh *ají limo*, seeds removed, chopped

1 tbsp. honey

Make the Yuzu Honey Ají Limo Dressing: Place the yuzu juice and ají limo in a blender and mix well. Add the honey and pulse to blend.

Customizing parties the Nobu way can be real fun! We always go all out to please our guests. *Nigiri-zushi* hand-prepared on the spot, sizzling skewers at the barbecue counter, mixed rice cooked in earthenware pots, *udon* noodles, even racks of lamb—this beats the spread at any top restaurant! Food and drinks, hot and cold—our staff has to be in top form to make sure everything is served just right. —*N.M.*

KUSHIYAKI WITH SHISO CHIMICHURRI AND ANTICUCHO

In Japan, skewers are called *kushi*, hence *kushiyaki* "tidbits grilled on skewers" and *kushiage* "tidbits deep-fried on skewers," both of which are very common fare at *izakaya* pubs and *yatai* food stalls. So I was happy to come across *anticuchos* in Peru. The street vendors there typically serve beef heart and organ meats with red and yellow salsas as shown on the two skewers in the foreground, but we've added a green *chimichurri* salsa from Argentina that uses lots of Japanese *shiso* and Peruvian *huacatay*—distant cousins to basil and mint. Our ingredients include (from the front) *tsukune* ground chicken, hearts of palm, wagyu beef and beets. Then we use quality *binchotan* oak charcoal, highly regarded by Japanese kushiyaki chefs for its even infrared heat, and slowly, slowly grill the skewers until done just so. —*N.M.*

6 sugarcane skewers and 18 bamboo skewers for serving

Chicken Tsukune

1 lb. (450 g) minced chicken

1 thumb-size knob ginger, grated

½ tsp. garlic purée

2 tbsp. potato starch

2 tbsp. soy sauce

¼ tsp. freshly ground black pepper

2 tsp. minced scallion

1 tsp. *yuzu*-pepper paste (*yuzu-kosho*)

Wagyu Skewers

1 lb. (450 g) wagyu beef steak

3 to 6 fresh shiitake mushrooms

9 baby red beets

6 to 8 fresh small hearts of palm

4 tbsp. Shiso Chimichurri Sauce (p. 184)

4 tbsp. Yellow Anticucho Sauce (p. 57)

4 tbsp. Red Anticucho Sauce (p. 184)

Extra-virgin olive oil

Salt and pepper

Chives, thinly sliced (optional)

1. Combine all Chicken Tsukune ingredients in a bowl. With wet hands, divide the chicken into 6 and press onto the sugarcane skewers.

2. Cut the beef into 18 bite-size cubes. Cut the shiitake mushrooms into 12 bite-size pieces. Thread 3 beef cubes and 2 shiitake mushrooms alternately on 6 bamboo skewers.

3. Peel and cut the beets in half and thread 3 halves on 6 bamboo skewers.

4. Cut the hearts of palm into 24 bite-size pieces. If large and thick, slice in half make 24 bite-size pieces. Thread 4 pieces onto 6 bamboo skewers.

5. Season all of the skewers except the chicken with salt, pepper, and olive oil. Grill over high heat.

6. Serve the Shiso Chimichurri, Yellow Anticucho Sauce and Red Anticucho sauce in dipping cups, or spoon over the skewers. Sprinkle with chives.

BAHAMIAN CONCH SALAD, NOBU STYLE

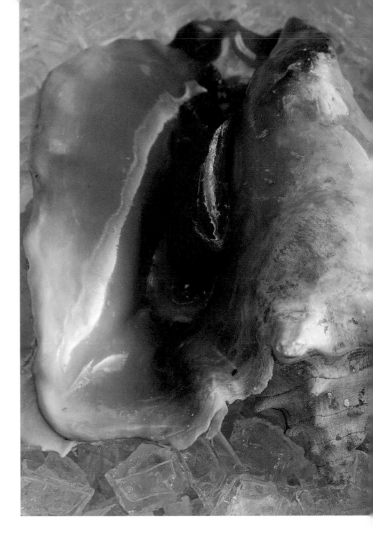

Thomas gives me a sly grin and says, "Remember when we went to that conch stand in the Bahamas with the Nobu chefs? Well, three of them ended up having children at the same time!" (In fact, one of those new fathers just happens to be Thomas.) That's right, conch is said to be a potent aphrodisiac. Here, then, is a ceviche that uses conch, although marinated much less than in most traditional ceviche recipes because we want the fresh, chewy textures and flavors to shine through. Pass it around in a large bowl with serving spoons so your guests can help themselves. —*N.M.*

MAKES 10 PORTIONS

1 queen conch, shucked and cleaned
½ orange bell pepper, seeded and diced
½ green bell pepper, seeded and diced
1 red onion, diced finely
2 medium tomatoes, peeled, seeded, and diced
¼ tsp. chopped scotch bonnet pepper
½ tbsp. chopped cilantro
2 tsp. salt
Juice of 4 limes
Juice of 3 oranges
1 tbsp. *yuzu* juice
Cilantro leaves, as garnish

Pound the conch to tenderize, then cut into bite-size pieces. Mix all vegetables with the conch, salt, and citrus juices. Place the conch salad in a serving bowl and garnish with the cilantro leaves.

Some streets in the Bahamas are lined with conch stands that serve up the freshest conch salad imaginable. Every Bahamian man has a favorite stand that he visits at least once a day. Going back and forth between Miami and Nassau as I do, I soon found my own favorite. I take my seat on a stool, beer in hand, and watch how quickly the local cooks can extract the meat from those impossibly convoluted shells. Such amazing skill! Conch meat is tougher than scallops or pen shells, so it must first be tenderized by pounding with the flat of a knife. Marinating in vinegar makes it even more tender. —*T.B.*

CRACKED CONCH, NOBU STYLE

Conch salad, conch stew, conch chowder, conch fritters, cracked conch . . . there's no end of conch dishes in the Bahamas. Here we take cracked conch tenderized with a meat mallet, coat it with the Rum Tempura Batter and deep-fry it. All very simple, served piping hot from the fryer with coarse sea salt and fresh-ground black pepper—what could be better? Well, this time we made a special green apple aioli dipping sauce that brings the natural succulence of the conch meat into even sharper focus. —*T.B.*

10 slices queen conch, tenderized

1 cup (240 ml) Rum Tempura Batter
(See p. 183 and substitute rum for water)

1 tbsp. all-purpose flour

Vegetable oil for frying

$\frac{1}{2}$ cup (120 ml) Apple Aioli (recipe follows)

1 tsp. chopped chives

Sea salt and freshly ground black pepper, for serving

1. Dust the conch slices with flour, dip into the Rum Tempura Batter, and fry at 360 °F (180 °C) until golden brown. Transfer to a paper-lined dish to drain any excess oil.

2. Arrange the conch fries on a platter. Place the apple aioli into individual dipping cups and garnish with chives. Mound the sea salt and pepper on the side.

APPLE AIOLI   MAKES 1 CUP (240 ML)

1 green apple, peeled, cored and cut into chunks

1 tbsp. rice vinegar

1 tsp. lemon juice

$1\frac{1}{2}$ tbsp. mayonnaise

Place the apple chunks, vinegar and lemon juice in a non-reactive saucepan over low heat and cook until soft. Place in a blender and mix into a purée. Transfer to a bowl and allow to cool slightly. Add the mayonnaise while still warm. Set aside.

WAGYU RIB-EYE TOBANYAKI

Cooking ever so slowly on a solid ceramic *toban* ensures an even heat that penetrates the center of every ingredient. In Japan we typically invite friends over to cook crab or meat this way on a tabletop brazier at home, but it's perfect for intimate parties too. Here we've cooked a whole round of rib-eye, then sliced it for presentation, but you can also cook thin slices right on the *toban*. Either way, you want to serve it to your guests while it's hot off the plate. —*N.M.*

SERVES 2, OR 4 AS AN APPETIZER

1 *toban* earthenware dish, for cooking and serving

1 ribeye cap, about 10 oz. (300 g)
Salt and freshly ground black pepper
2 tsp. olive oil
Selection of baby vegetables, such as carrots, turnips, beets, radishes, shiitake
    mushrooms and zucchini, blanched

1 tbsp. unsalted butter
2 tbsp. sake

Yuzu Soy (mix in advance)
4 tsp. soy sauce
2 tsp. *yuzu* juice

1. Season the ribeye cap generously with salt.

2. Trim the vegetables, as needed, and blanch in salted boiling water. Shock in ice water and drain.

3. Grill the ribeye cap until the surface is browned, about 4 minutes for each side. Allow to rest for 15 minutes and cut into slices. Alternatively, sear the ribeye cap in a large hot frying pan with 2 tsp. olive oil. Remember that the meat will continue to cook a little in the toban dish later, so you should cook it slightly rarer than you would eat normally.

4. Place the toban dish on an open flame. Put in the meat, surround with the vegetables and add the butter. When the butter sizzles, add the sake, being careful in case the alcohol ignites. Add the Yuzu Soy and cover with a lid. Serve immediately.

Blood Orange Martini (see p. 189 for recipe)

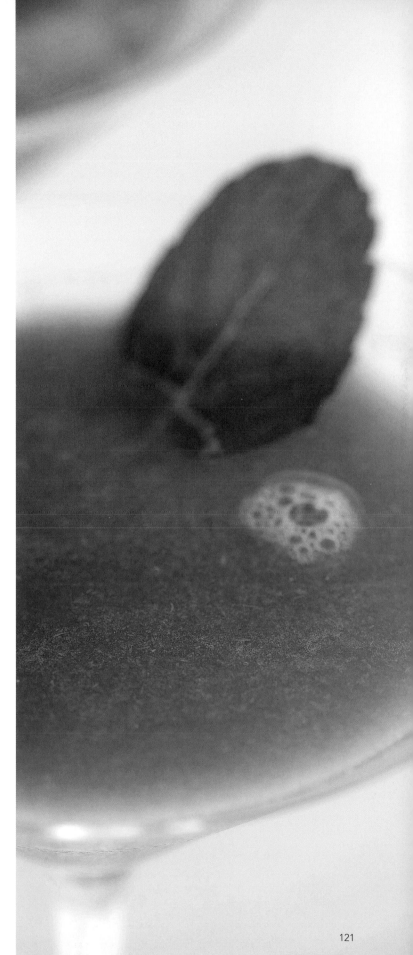

ROASTED POUSSIN WITH WASABI SAUCE

This dish comes from Nobu London, where I worked before coming to Miami. There we used cabbage for stuffing, but for my new version I use wild rice and make a risotto with onion, garlic and green bell peppers—real Latin-Caribbean basics. The trick is not to hurry—how very Latin!—it takes time to draw out all the sweetness of the vegetables. You won't believe how well the crispy *poussin* skin goes with this mild and mellow wild rice. —*T.B.*

MAKES 1 WHOLE BABY CHICKEN

Wasabi Sauce
4 tbsp. (30 g) wasabi powder
3⅓ tbsp. soy sauce
3 tbsp. light soy sauce
1 tsp. unsalted butter
½ tsp. roughly ground black pepper

1½ cups wild rice
3 cups water
¼ small green bell pepper, minced
⅛ medium yellow onion, minced
1 clove garlic, minced
1 cup (240 ml) Dashi Stock, or more (p.183)

1 whole Cornish hen (*poussin*), boned
Sea salt and freshly ground black pepper
Pure olive oil
2 tsp. preserved capers, chopped
6 to 8 tender inner leaves of Savoy cabbage

1. Make the Wasabi Sauce: mix the wasabi powder in an equal amount of water to form a smooth paste. Cover and allow to stand for 12 minutes to develop its fiery flavor. Add the soy sauces mix well, and transfer to a small saucepan. Place the pan over low heat to gently cook. Add the butter and pepper and stir. The sauce should be runny. If the sauce is too thick, add some dashi or water to adjust consistency.

2. Preheat the oven to 500°F (260°C).

3. Place the wild rice and water in a saucepan, cover and bring to a simmer. Cook for 25 to 30 minutes until almost done (it will be finished later).

4. Place the bell pepper, onion, garlic and olive oil in a frying pan over medium-low heat. Cook, without browning, until soft. Combine with the cooked rice in a pot and add the dashi stock. Cook over low heat for 10 minutes. Cool to room temperature.

5. Lightly rinse the hen and blot dry, including inside the body cavity. Season the inside of the hen with salt and pepper. Carefully line the cavity with the cabbage, then stuff with the wild rice mixture. Place a skewer through the back legs and front wings to hold them in place. Place on a sheet tray over a roasting rack and rub the hen all over with olive oil, salt and pepper.

6. Roast the hen in the oven for 15 to 20 minutes total. During roasting, rotate the hen if needed. Remove from the oven. The skin should be quite crispy and the rice filling should be hot. Allow to rest for 5 minutes.

7. Cut the hen in half and arrange on a platter. Mix the Wasabi Sauce with the capers and serve on the side.

GREGORIO'S ARTICHOKE NOODLE SALAD

Pasta is a must for casual lunch parties. This recipe is something Gregorio, the chef at Nobu Malibu, came up with when he wanted to explore Nobu-style possibilities in pasta. He brilliantly combined an abundance of baby artichoke shavings with Inaniwa *udon* noodles to make a salad-like dish that is healthy and light, but packed with Japanese and Italian *umami* flavors. Our White Dry Miso is Kyoto sweet white miso that's been oven-dried, then likewise blended with parmesan cheese, which has some of the same flavor compounds. You just know it has to taste great! —*T.B.*

Inaniwa *udon* noodles, made from wheat, salt and water, are a special product made in Akita, in the north of Japan. Of the many brands, we prefer to use Sato Yosuke Shoten's handmade noodles at Nobu. You can really taste the difference. They're prepared with such loving attention, you can feel the warmth in each bite. As with other pasta, the secret is to heat plenty of water and only add the dry pasta when it reaches a rolling boil, then drain the noodles as soon as they turn clear and rinse off the surface starch repeatedly with cold water. In Japan, we call this "tightening" the noodles. It leaves the surface squeaky clean and gives the udon a nice bite. —*N.M.*

8 oz. (220 g) Inaniwa *udon* noodles

⅔ cup (60 g) sliced leeks

Vegetable oil for frying

35 baby artichokes

2 sprigs parsley (or lemon slices)

1 tbsp. olive oil

1 tsp. truffle oil

½ tbsp. *yuzu* juice

3 pinches freshly ground pepper

1 tbsp. White Dry Miso (p. 134)

1 tbsp. grated Parmesan cheese

Pinch salt

1 tbsp. Yuzu Dressing (recipe follows)

1. Cook the noodles in boiling water for about 3 minutes, drain and rinse in cold water to remove excess starch. Drain and set aside.

2. Deep-fry the leeks at 320 °F (160 °C) until crisp. Set aside.

3. Trim the artichokes and slice paper-thin. Place in water with parsley (or lemon) in it to prevent discoloration. Dry the artichokes by squeezing them gently in a towel. Dress with the olive oil, truffle oil, yuzu juice, ground pepper, White Dry Miso and Parmesan cheese. Season with a pinch of salt (more to taste). Mix in half of the fried leeks.

4. Toss the noodles in the Yuzu Dressing and top with the artichoke salad. Garnish with the remaining leeks.

YUZU DRESSING
MAKES ABOUT 1¼ CUPS (310 ML)

6 tbsp. *yuzu* juice

2⅔ tbsp. soy sauce

1 tsp. freshly ground black pepper

1 tsp. garlic purée

¾ cup (180 ml) grapeseed oil

Whisk all ingredients together.

ARROZ CON FRUTAS DE MAR

I used to dislike cilantro. Then one day, I was invited to a Peruvian home for *arroz con pollo*—very simply, rice cooked with chicken—but they mixed in lots of cilantro! Arroz con pollo is served at celebrations in Peru, and there I was, the guest of honor, so I couldn't very well *not* eat it. I remember struggling to clean my plate. People's tastes change, however, and now I really love cilantro. Here, then, is our Miami seafood rice—not quite the same thing, but equally memorable. How can rice cooked with seafood broth taste so good? Could it be that secret hint of beer? —*N.M.*

MAKES 6 PORTIONS

1 large *donabe* pot or heavy pot for cooking (4 qt./4 L capacity)

Frutas de Mar

10 bay scallops

1 red mullet, filleted and boned

6 pink shrimp, shelled and deveined

2 baby octopus, cleaned

3 whole calamari, cleaned

1 large stone crab claw, shelled

1 piece *kombu*, 2 in. (5 cm) square

2½ cups (500 g) short-grain rice, washed and drained

9 sprigs cilantro, separated into stems and leaves

1 tbsp. sliced garlic in olive oil

A few slices of ají limo, or any hot pepper

1 cup (240 ml) Dashi Stock (p. 183)

1½ cups (360 ml) Nobu beer (lagar or ale works well)

1 tsp. salt

¼ tsp. pepper

1. Cut the seafood into bite-size pieces.

2. Place the kombu at the bottom of the donabe pot. Add half the rice, the cilantro stems, the rest of the rice, and the cilantro leaves. Top with the garlic and ají limo (or hot pepper).

3. Place the seafood on the rice and add the dashi stock, beer, salt and pepper.

4. Cover the pot with a heavy lid and bring to a boil over high heat. When steam begins to escape, or when you hear a boiling sound, reduce the heat to medium-low. Continue to cook 10 to 12 minutes without opening the lid.

5. Turn heat to medium-high and cook a further 7 minutes. Do not open the lid.

6. Turn heat to high for 10 seconds, then turn off heat. Wait 15 minutes to allow the rice steam evenly before removing the lid.

7. Using a spatula or a Japanese rice paddle, gently fold the rice, bringing the cooked grains from bottom to top to release the steam. Arrange into individual bowls.

Automatic rice cookers are extremely convenient and popular, through recently more and more Japanese are going back to cooking rice in ceramic pots. There are regional clays and pottery styles to meet every personal preference, but the important thing to look for when buying one is a heavy, tight lid and a thick bottom that transmits even heat. And there's the added plus when cooking rice in ceramic: at the bottom of the pot, you get a nice crisp *okoge* crust, a childhood favorite for many Japanese. That toasty fragrance really takes me back. —*N.M.*

INTIMATE DINNERS

PUMPKIN MINI-CHAWAN MUSHI

Chawan mushi is a savory Japanese cus-tard made from egg and *dashi* stock. The egg mixture is steamed to a creamy yoghurt-like smoothness that just melts in your mouth, leaving only a heartwarming flavor—the perfect starter for an intimate dinner. It takes practice to get the timing just right: steam it too long and the egg will get firm and spongy, so you really have to know your steamer. Here we've hollowed out miniature squash so you can eat the insides with a spoon, but any nicely designed heat-resistant cups that can be brought straight to the table make a delightful visual treat. —*T.B.*

MAKES 6 SMALL CUPS

6 mini honey squash (or small heat-proof cups)

¼ *kabocha* pumpkin, about 10 oz. (280 g), peeled and seeded

1 tsp. unsalted butter

3 large eggs, lightly beaten

2 cups (480 ml) Dashi Stock (p. 183)

1 tsp. light soy sauce

1 tsp. *mirin*

Pinch salt

Olive oil for sautéing

Salt and pepper

2 tbsp. Gin-an (p. 140)

¼ cup (20 g) trumpet mushrooms, blanched (optional)

Extra-virgin olive oil (optional)

1. Cut the tops off the mini-squash to make a lid and scoop out the pulp to form a cup. Trim the bottoms so that they sit flat. Set aside.

2. Cut four ¼ in. (6 mm)-thick slices from the kabocha pumpkin and reserve for step 5. Cut the rest into chunks and place in a pot with the butter. Add enough water to barely cover the pumpkin. Bring to a gentle simmer, cover, and cook until soft. Drain and purée in a blender. Set aside.

3. Combine the dashi, light soy sauce, mirin and salt. Mix gently with the egg. Avoid whisking, as this incorporates too much air. Gently stir in the pumpkin purée.

4. Pour the mixture into the mini-squash cups. Place the cups in a steamer, cover, and gently steam for 15 minutes. To prevent condensation from dripping on the food, the lid can be covered with a kitchen towel.

5. Meanwhile, dice the reserved pumpkin slices and sauté in a little olive oil. Season with salt and pepper.

6. Place the chawan mushi on a serving plate and top with some of the diced pumpkin and mushrooms, if using. Spoon the Gin-an over. Garnish the plate with the diced pumpkin and several drops of extra-virgin olive oil.

STEAMED CHILEAN SEA BASS WITH DRY MISO

This is the cooked version of our ever-popular Nobu Sashimi with Dry Miso. Other lean fish—cod, halibut, turbot, snapper, grouper—can be used, but the important thing is to get the thickest fillet you can find. You want something you can sink your teeth into. Line a steamer with *kombu* kelp, place the fillet on top, and steam. Make sure, of course, not to cook it too much—just until it flakes when you insert a fork or chopstick. Transfer the steamed fish to a serving dish and smother with plenty of dried miso, enough to hide the skin, so it's sandwiched between layers of *umami*. Delicious top to bottom.　—*N.M.*

Ginger and Lychee Martini (see p. 189 for recipe)

(see p. 189 for recipe)

SERVES 6

6 Chilean sea bass fillets, 6 oz. (170 g) each, skin-off

Sea salt

6 pieces dried *kombu*, each 4 in. (10 cm) square

1 qt. (1 L) sake

½ cup (80 g) White Dry Miso (recipe follows; use white miso)

½ cup (80 g) Red Dry Miso (recipe follows; use red miso)

6 tsp. *yuzu* juice

6 tsp. extra-virgin olive oil

Garlic Chips (p. 183)

Chives, as garnish

1. Sprinkle each fillet with a little sea salt. Place the kombu on a tray and top each square with a fillet. Pour the sake over, cover with plastic wrap and set in a steamer. Steam until the fillets are just cooked, 10 to 15 minutes, depending on the thickness of the fish.

2. Arrange the fillets with the kombu on a warm serving plate. Drizzle the fish with a little yuzu juice and olive oil. Cover the fish with the White Dry Miso and Red Dry Miso. Top with Garlic Chips and chives.

DRY MISO　　　　　　　　MAKES ABOUT ½ CUP (80 G)

⅔ cup (180 g) miso (any type of cooking miso such as red, white and yellow works well)

Using a palette knife, spread the miso as thinly as possible on a non-stick baking mat. Place in a warm area to dry out naturally, for 1 to 2 days. Alternatively, dry in a 230 °F (110 °C) oven for 1 to 2 hours, being careful not to allow the miso to darken. Crumble evenly. Keep in an air-tight container.

Florida is close to the Bahamas. We also have the "Nobu Atlantis, Paradise Island" restaurant in Nassau, which can seat over 180. With a casino on the premises, we always get a houseful of guests who are hungry after gambling (or before!).

The Bahamas crowd like their seafood. All kinds of snapper and coralfish, a full array of colorful fish that reminds Nobu of the catch in Okinawa. Most are white-fleshed and very tender, so I often chill them with ice for slicing. Bahamian fish are especially good pan-seared.

And let's not forget conch—a must-try in the Bahamas. Of course we also serve conchs in Miami. We also get spiny lobsters and huge crabs, prime ingredients for that festive note on our menus.

In the back of Nobu Atlantis we also have a special sake room with a more classic Nobu atmosphere. I helped plan the kitchen and restaurant layout. We had different designers for Miami and Nassau, so each is totally unique. I now shuttle back and forth between the two locations, but I'm quite fond of them both. —T.B.

CEVICHE SOUP

I think the best soups are those that give pride of place to the local produce, letting those special regional flavors shine through. That's especially important with seafood, so here's my quick course in the flavors of Florida's coastal waters coastal waters— stone crab claws, squid, clam, mussels, mullet, pink shrimp. All of them make for an unbelievable broth! And since we're so close to South America, add a squeeze of sour lime to spread through this sumptuous sea and really bring home the essence of the catch. The perfect soup to start a dinner. —*T.B.*

SERVES 6

Selection of seafood, such as:
6 Florida clams
6 mussels
6 Key Largo pink shrimp
6 baby squid
1 red mullet
6 stone crab claws, shells removed

4 tbsp. sake for cooking clams and mussels
2¼ qt. (2.2 L) Dashi Stock (p. 183)
Salt

1 tbsp. light soy sauce
Juice of 5 key limes
2 to 3 bird's-eye chili peppers, stemmed

½ red onion, finely sliced
5 tbsp. chopped cilantro
1½ cups (360 ml) sake

1. Clean and fillet the seafood as needed.

2. Place a frying pan over high heat. Add the clams and 2 tbsp. sake and cover. Cook until the clams start to open. Transfer the clams to a bowl with their liquid. Repeat with the mussels. Discard any unopened shells.

3. In a pot, mix the dashi, salt, soy sauce, lime juice and chili peppers and bring to a simmer. Add the shrimp, then the squid. Cook for 2 minutes. Add the mullet and cook a further 2 minutes. Add in sequence the crab, clams, mussels, then onion and cilantro. Bring to a gentle simmer and remove from heat.

4. Remove the cooked chili peppers. Divide the soup among 6 bowls.

UNI-CRUSTED FLORIDA SPINY LOBSTER

Different countries pride themselves on their lobster, each saying the local catch is the best. At Nobu, we do sometimes use big-clawed Maine lobsters, but let's not overlook Florida spiny lobsters. First simmered slowly in *kombu dashi*, then slathered with Nobu's own *uni* sea urchin butter and oven-broiled until the skin just begins to char and gives off such a sublime aroma! Even if you're serving individual portions, a platter of whole lobsters makes quite an impact. Squeeze lots of key lime over top! —*T.B.*

SERVES 6

Uni Butter
4 tbsp. *uni* sea urchin
6 tbsp. unsalted butter
4 tsp. light soy sauce
Zest and juice from 1 lemon
2 tbsp. *panko*
2 tsp. white miso

3 live spiny lobsters, about 14 oz. (400 g) each
3 small hearts of palm, cut into ¼ in. (6 mm) thick rounds
6 tbsp. Gin-an (recipe follows)
3 key limes, halved
1 piece *kombu*, 4 in. (10 cm) square

1. Make the Uni Butter: combine all ingredients in a blender. Set aside.

2. Place the kombu in a large pot of water and bring to a boil. Add the lobsters and cook for 12 minutes.

3. Cut the tails in half lengthwise. Clean and cut tail meat into bite-size pieces, then return the meat to the shells.

4. Cover each tail half with Uni Butter and bake at 450 °F (230 °C) until the surface becomes nicely golden brown.

5. Grill the hearts of palm and dress with the Gin-an.

6. Arrange the lobster on a platter or individual plates and place the hearts of palm and key lime on the side.

GIN-AN
MAKES SCANT 1 CUP (200 ML)

⅔ cup (180 ml) Dashi Stock (p. 183)
1 tbsp. sake
1 tbsp. light soy sauce

Pinch sea salt
1 tsp. *kudzu*, dissolved with 1 tsp. water

Combine all ingredients except the kudzu slurry in a saucepan and bring to a gentle simmer. Add the kudzu slurry to thicken, stir, and remove from heat.

S low-cooking at temperatures lower than what is usually called "poaching" is essential here; we don't want the *foie gras* to come to a boil and let all the fat melt away. A steady 110–160 °F (60–70 °C) for around 30 minutes—more or less depending on your cooktop—should be just about right. For the cooking liquid, we've mixed equal amounts of pinot noir, *umeshu* plum wine and *mirin* cooking sake, but if you can't find *umeshu* or *mirin*, which add a mellow sweetness, a tawny port will do nicely. Enjoy the exquisite buttery texture on rice crackers—and if you have some high-quality coarse salt, sprinkle it on top. —*N.M.*

SERVES 6

1 whole *foie gras*, grade A, as-is (uncleaned)
Salt and freshly ground black pepper
3 cups (720 ml) pinot noir
3 cups (720 ml) plum wine

3 cups (720 ml) *mirin*
1 lb. (450 g) red seedless grapes
Rice Crackers (recipe follows)
Sea salt for finishing
Chives, as garnish

1. Season foie gras with salt and pepper. Sear on a very hot grill or grill pan, just enough to mark both sides well.

2. Bring the pinot noir, plum wine, mirin and grapes to a boil in a saucepan, then cool to 140 °F (60 °C). Add the foie gras and cook for 30 minutes, maintaining a temperature of 140 °F (60 °C).

3. Remove the foie gras and cool to room temperature. Reserve the grapes and cooking liquid.

4. Slice the foie gras into ½ in. (1.5 cm)-thick pieces. Serve with the grapes and a few spoonfuls of the cooking liquid. Sprinkle sea salt over top. Garnish with the chives.

RICE CRACKERS

2 cups (370 g) Cooked Rice (p. 184)
½ cup (120 ml) water
1 tsp. salt

1. Place the rice, salt and cold water in a pot and re-cook until the grains become soft and slightly mushy. Cook dry. Roll in foil into cylinders and freeze.

2. Slice into rounds on a slicing machine and dry overnight on a non-stick silicone mat.

3. Keep in an airtight container. When needed, deep-fry in oil at 200 °F (93 °C) until the rice puffs up. Transfer to a paper-lined dish to drain any excess oil.

MARINATED GRILLED SHORT RIBS

Dig into these spicy-sour marinated ribs with your hands. Finger-licking irresistible! Taking a hint from the sesame paste and meat juice dipping sauce they make in Japan, here I've made a macadamia dipping sauce rich with the nutty flavor of the natural oil. Then for contrast, a bonito-based sauce from the Japanese bonito fishing region of Tosa, sharpened with a brisk dash of rice vinegar.

—T.B.

MAKES 10 RIBS

10 short ribs, trimmed

Marinade
½ cup (120 ml) sake
½ cup (120 ml) *mirin*
¼ cups (60 ml) soy sauce
2 slices ginger
½ dried chili pepper
1 tsp. black peppercorns

1 leek, tender part only, cleaned and julienned
2 scallions, finely sliced, washed and blotted dry
1 tbsp. Momiji Oroshi (p. 183)
¼ cup (60 ml) Shallot Tosazu (p. 184)
¼ cup (60 ml) Macadamia Sauce (p. 184)
1 fresh *ají limo*, or any red chili pepper, finely sliced
1 tsp. sesame seeds
Pinch sea salt

1. Mix all marinade ingredients in a bowl. Dress the short ribs with the marinade and refrigerate overnight or at least 8 hours.

2. Remove the ribs from the marinade. Reserve the marinade. Heat the grill over medium-high flame so as not to char the ribs. Cook the ribs gently, turning when nicely caramelized.

3. Meanwhile, in a small saucepan over medium-low heat, reduce the marinade to a syrupy consistency.

4. Soak the julienned leek in ice water to crisp and remove bitterness.

5. Mound the short ribs on a serving platter and sprinkle with the chilis, sesame seeds and salt. Top with the leek. Serve the Shallot Tosazu and Macadamia Sauce in separate dipping cups, with the scallions and Momiji Oroshi alongside.

ROAST DUCK AND CONFIT "HAVANA CLUB"

This venture into "serious cooking" requires lots of ingredients and may or may not please everyone—though our Miami guests all seem to enjoy it. Preparation involves crumbling unwrapped Cuban cigars over a *binchotan* oak charcoal brazier until they give off a marvelous tobacco perfume. The idea came from *hobayaki*, a Japanese regional dish in which dried *hoba* magnolia leaves topped with miso—sometimes with mushrooms, peppers, duck or even wagyu beef—are roasted on a brazier until the miso bubbles and the toasted leaf imparts a special fragrance to the food. *Haute cuisine* for all the senses, not least the sense of smell. —*T.B.*

SERVES 6

Duck Leg Confit

6 duck legs

½ cup (120 ml) *moromi* miso

2 oranges, zest finely grated and remaining pulp juiced

6 cups (1 kg) duck fat (optional)

Sauce

¼ cup (60 ml) Veal Stock (p. 184) (beef stock, brown chicken stock or water can be substituted)

1 cup (240 ml) Aka Den Miso (p. 184)

1 tbsp. dark rum

1 tobacco leaf, from the outside of the cigar

1 tbsp. chopped tarragon

1 duck breast

Salt and freshly ground black pepper

1 Asian pear (*nashi*), cut into 6 tournée

2 cups (480 ml) Simple Syrup (p. 185)

2 tsp. salt

4 heads baby bok choy, steamed

⅔ cup (160 ml) Mango Salsa (p. 185)

6 *hoba* magnolia leaves, dried

1. Marinate the duck legs overnight in the mixture of moromi miso, orange zest and juice. Place the duck legs in a *sous-vide* bag along with the marinade, and cook in 180 °F/82 °C water for 9 hours. Set aside. While warm, wipe off the marinade and remove the bones. Trim the meat and cut into pieces.

2. If you don't have sous-vide equipment, heat oven to 275 °F (135 °C). Melt 6 cups (1 kg) duck fat in a flat-bottomed pan. Remove the duck legs from the marinade and wipe clean. Place the legs in the pan over low heat and cook, uncovered, for 3½ to 4 hours. The legs should be very tender. Leave to cool in the fat. Remove the bones while the meat is still warm. Trim the legs and cut into pieces.

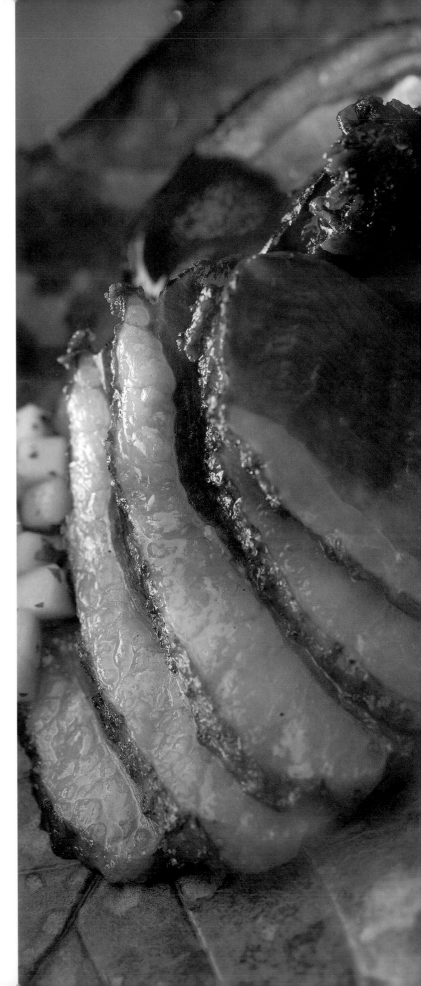

3. Mix the veal stock and Aka Den Miso in a saucepan and place over low heat. Add a pinch tobacco leaf and tarragon to infuse. Place a frying pan over medium heat, add the rum, and flame. Add flamed run to sauce. Strain and set aside.

4. Season the duck breast with salt and pepper and place into a hot sauté pan, skin side down. Sear the skin to achieve a nice golden color and to crisp, about 6 minutes. Turn it over and cook for 3 minutes more. Transfer to a warm plate and allow to rest.

5. Place the duck leg pieces, skin side up, on a sheet pan. Spoon a little veal stock over and put into an oven at 400 °F (200 °C) to brown.

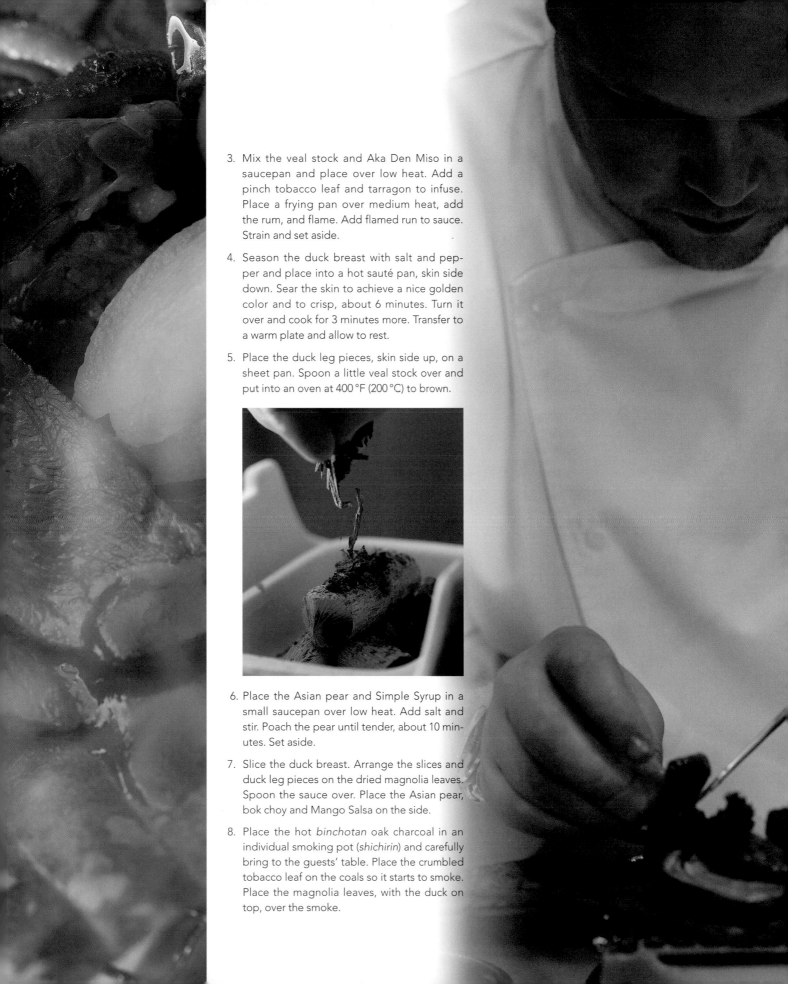

6. Place the Asian pear and Simple Syrup in a small saucepan over low heat. Add salt and stir. Poach the pear until tender, about 10 minutes. Set aside.

7. Slice the duck breast. Arrange the slices and duck leg pieces on the dried magnolia leaves. Spoon the sauce over. Place the Asian pear, bok choy and Mango Salsa on the side.

8. Place the hot *binchotan* oak charcoal in an individual smoking pot (*shichirin*) and carefully bring to the guests' table. Place the crumbled tobacco leaf on the coals so it starts to smoke. Place the magnolia leaves, with the duck on top, over the smoke.

I got into the world of sushi thinking it would be glamorous—was I ever wrong! I didn't even get to touch sushi while apprenticing. For three years, it was all cleaning shop and washing dishes and running deliveries.

My wages were so low I couldn't even afford a knife, but an older apprentice gave me one of his. The blade was really worn, but I sharpened it diligently. I'd had a job sharpening hand tools in a factory before, so I knew how to use a whetstone. Unfortunately, I did such a good job that the man took back his beautifully reconditioned knife.

Plenty of times I wanted to give up, but I'd always spring back. I knew better than to let things get to me. When my restaurant in Alaska burned to the ground, a great many people came to my rescue, no doubt because I didn't throw in the towel.

You just can't give up the restaurant business. You always have to keep thinking, how can we make this better? It's all hands-on, you've got to actively evolve and transform. If you fail, well, people can forgive that—but not before you try your best. Fail and fail again, you just have to keep trying. That's my life up to now, and from here on as well. —*N.M.*

NOBU CLASSICS

ANKIMO WITH ROASTED RED PEPPER MISO

*A*nko, or monkfish, is highly prized in Japan, on par with *fugu* blowfish. An ugly-looking creature, its liver or *kimo* is especially valued by *kaiseki* masters and sushi chefs alike. At Tsukiji and other fish markets, the size of the liver is what determines the price for the whole fish. Steamed fatty winter monkfish liver rivals *foie gras* for gelatinous richness and a creamy smooth texture that many find irresistible. Here we liven it up with an unconventional twist: a roasted red pepper miso sauce that combines sweet and savory, fresh and fermented in a swirl of sophisticated flavors. The yellow shoot used for garnish is a recent Nobu discovery, a sugar-sweet micro-cultivar—any guesses? —*N.M.*

MAKES 6 PORTIONS

Red Pepper Miso Sauce

6 medium red bell peppers

Salt and pepper

Olive oil for brushing peppers

2 tbsp. rice vinegar

2 spring onion bulbs, sliced

1 cup (240 ml) Den Miso (p. 156)

10½ oz. (300 g) *ankimo* monk fish liver

1 qt. (1 L) water

2 tbsp. (30 g) salt

3 cups (720 ml) sake

1 oz. (30 g) caviar (Osetra)

Baby chives, as garnish

Corn shoots, as garnish

1. Make the Red Pepper Miso Sauce: Cut the red bell peppers in half lengthwise and remove the seeds. Season with salt and pepper and brush with olive oil. Roast skin-side up in a 450 °F (230 °C) oven until the skin blisters and turns dark. Peel and remove the skin while hot. Put the peeled peppers, rice vinegar and spring onions in a blender and mix until smooth. Add the Den Miso and blend until combined.

2. Peel off the thin membrane around the liver and remove the blood vessels with a pair of tweezers. Combine the salt and water in a pot and soak the liver for 20 to 30 minutes to remove the blood. Rinse and soak in sake for 2 minutes. Cut into chunks and pat dry with paper towel.

3. Lay plastic wrap on a flat surface. Place the liver on top and roll into a cylindrical shape about 2 in. (5 cm) in diameter. Poke air holes with a bamboo skewer to allow any liquid to drain during steaming. Roll the liver in aluminum foil to hold its shape during steaming. Seal at both ends. Wrap in a bamboo rolling mat and secure with a rubber band.

4. Place the roll in a steamer and steam for 40 to 50 minutes. Remove from the steamer and allow to cool to room temperature in the bamboo mat. Refrigerate.

5. Unwrap the bamboo mat and cut the liver roll into 6 pieces, about 1¼ in. (3 cm) each. Make sure to remove all of the plastic wrap and foil. Spoon the Red Pepper Miso Sauce onto each serving plate and top with a liver round. Garnish with caviar, chives and corn shoots.

TILEFISH SASHIMI SALAD WITH MATSUHISA DRESSING

ere we pair up the eternal Nobu classic Sashimi Salad with my minced onion-soy sauce Matsuhisa Dressing. Lately it's become easier to get various high-quality micro greens in America, mostly for use as a garnish, though it is a great waste to let them go limp in the refrigerator. These micro greens may be tiny, but they're alive and breathing and full of distinctive flavors—sharp and pungent and sweet and crisp. Their inner energy really carries over to the fresh fish. —*N.M.*

SERVES 6

Matsuhisa Dressing

⅓ medium white onion, finely minced

2 tbsp. soy sauce

1 tbsp. rice vinegar

Pinch sugar

Pinch mustard powder

¼ tsp. freshly ground black pepper

1 tsp. sea salt

1 tsp. grapeseed oil

1 tsp. roasted sesame oil

4 oz. (120 g) tilefish fillet, cleaned and boned

3 cups (300 g) mixed micro greens

Cucumber, *udo*, carrot and candy beet, sliced peper-thin, as garnish (optional)

1. Make the Matsuhisa Dressing: Once the onion is minced, rinse in cold water and drain. Blot dry with a paper towel. Mix all ingredients except the oil. Add the oil and set aside.

2. Slice the tilefish thinly and roll up each slice. Dress the greens lightly with Matsuhisa Dressing and arrange on a plate. Place the fish around the greens and spoon the dressing around the fish. Garnish with the sliced vegetables.

BLACK SEA BASS WITH JALAPEÑO MISO

Black cod with miso is so well-known by now that we sometimes respond to special requests with variations that aren't on the menu. This South American take on the recipe inserts just a twist of tartness and spice by adding jalapeños to the miso marinade. Cod can be done this way, of course, but *toro* tuna belly, salmon, and even beef work well too. Don't rinse off the miso; just wipe away the excess and the coating will give off a mouth-watering roasted aroma. And while you're at it, grill the limes too! Even the most steadfast "Nobu standard" fans will love this one. —*T.B.*

MAKES 6 PORTIONS

Six 7 oz. (200 g) black sea bass fillets, boneless, skin-on

2 cups (480 ml) Den Miso (recipe follows)

12 jalapeños

3 key limes

6 Hajikami Ginger Shoot Pickles (recipe follows)

1. Seed half of the jalapeños. Dice both the seeded and unseeded jalapeños and place in a blender with the Den Miso. Mix until smooth.
2. Reserve a few tablespoons of miso for plating. Marinate the black sea bass in the rest of the miso for one full day.
3. Wipe the miso off the black sea bass. Broil the fish skin-side up until the skin is browned and crisp.
4. Cut the key limes in half and grill or broil until just singed.
5. Place each fillet on a plate, add a few dots of sauce around the fish, and garnish with a lime half and a Hajikami Ginger Pickle.

DEN MISO   MAKES ABOUT 3 CUPS (720 ML)

½ cup (120 ml) sake

½ cup (120 ml) *mirin*

1⅓ cups (360 g) white miso

¾ cup plus 3 tbsp. (180 g) granulated sugar

1. Place the sake and mirin in a saucepan and bring to a boil for 2 to 3 minutes to evaporate the alcohol. Turn down the heat and stir in the miso to dissolve completely. Turn up the heat and add the sugar in 2 to 3 batches, stirring constantly to dissolve, so the mixture does not burn.

2. Remove from heat and allow to cool to room temperature.

HAJIKAMI GINGER SHOOT PICKLES

Cut ginger shoots into 6 in. (15 cm) lengths. Bring water to a boil in a pot and add 1 tbsp. vinegar per 1 qt./1 L water. Blanch the ginger, drain and sprinkle generously with salt. Cool to room temperature, then marinate in 1 part Amazu (p. 183) and 1 part water for 12 hours.

How to send our guests home happy? The only way is the best way—by doing everything we can to serve superb food. That was my thinking when I opened Matsuhisa in 1987 with only seven staff members, myself included. No time to eat, and at the end of the day we had to wash piles of pots and dishes ourselves, never getting to sleep before 2:00 or 3:00 a.m.

Then up early in the morning to go shopping for fish and vegetables. In those days I had zero credit, so I had buy everything with cash. My wife was the one who really handled the finances. She made up for all my professional shortcomings.

Now with so many restaurants under my belt, people tend to think that all you really need is a location and capital, but all the money in the world won't buy you reliable staff.

Nobu employs 2000 people worldwide. When I open a new place, I give well-trained Nobu team members new roles. It's their job to inject Nobu *kokoro* into the new restaurant. The Nobu brand may already enjoy glowing success, but there are no shortcuts. Everyone involved has to understand the underlying hard work, the importance of building up professionalism step by step, based on mutual trust. That's what makes a restaurant. —*N.M.*

CREAMY SPICY KEY LARGO PINK SHRIMP

Fish and shellfish may go by the same name or even look the same in different parts of the world, but regional characteristics can be astounding. This is especially true of shrimp and prawns, with one variety or another being especially loved as the local favorite. In Japan I lean toward *kuruma ebi,* but in Florida I favor the so-called pink shrimp: beautiful in color, and just the right size for cooking. I wish I could advise you to use fresh raw shrimp, but I know most supermarkets just sell defrosted "raw" shrimp. If this is the case, you're better off buying frozen shrimp and defrosting them at home. —*N.M.*

MAKES 2 PORTIONS

Creamy Spicy Sauce (makes 1 ½ cups /360 ml)
3 egg yolks
2 tsp. rice vinegar
1 tsp. *yuzu* juice
Scant 1 cup (200 ml) grapeseed oil
1 tsp. salt
½ tsp. freshly ground white pepper
2 tsp. Chili Garlic Sauce (p. 185)

18 pink shrimp, shelled and deveined
2 cups (500 ml) Tempura Batter (p. 183)
½ cup (65 g) all-purpose flour
1 tbsp. chopped chives
2 *shishito* peppers
1 tsp. yuzu juice
Vegetable oil for frying

1. Make the Creamy Spicy Sauce: Beat the egg yolks until pale and add the vinegar and yuzu juice. Slowly beat in the oil to form an emulsion. Season with salt and pepper. Add the Chili Garlic Sauce and mix well.

2. Dredge the shrimp in flour, shake off excess, dip in batter, and deep-fry at 360 °F (180 °C). Drain the excess oil. Fry the shishito peppers briefly without batter and drain.

3. Toss the shrimp in Creamy Spicy Sauce and yuzu juice. Place the shrimp in a serving bowl, sprinkle with chives, and garnish with the fried shishito peppers.

FLORIDA SPINY LOBSTER SALAD WITH SPICY LEMON DRESSING

We originally invented this spicy lemon dressing to go with mushrooms, blending grated ginger with fresh-ground black pepper. It goes with everything—grilled foods, fried foods, fresh vegetables, salads. We use grapeseed oil, which gives it a clean, light taste. Americans tend to combine shellfish with butter, so this makes a nice healthy contrast. It's very popular, too. —*N.M.*

MAKES 1 SALAD

Spicy Lemon Dressing (makes about 1⅛ cups /270 ml)
Scant ½ cup (100 ml) lemon juice
3 tbsp. plus 1 tsp. soy sauce
1 heaping tsp. grated ginger
1 tsp. sea salt
½ tsp. black pepper
Scant ⅔ cup (150 ml) grapeseed oil

1 spiny lobster, about 2 lbs. (900 g)
3 oz. mixed salad greens
3 tbsp. Spicy Lemon Dressing (recipe above)
5 whole shiitake mushrooms, stems removed
6 Garlic Chips (recipe p. 183)
¼ tsp. sesame seeds

1. Make the Spicy Lemon Dressing: Whisk all the dressing ingredients together, except the oil, until the salt is completely dissolved. Slowly add the oil, whisking constantly, until all of the oil is combined. Whisk a few more seconds to create a creamy emulsion.

2. Bring a pot of water to a boil and boil the lobster for exactly 12 minutes (spiny lobster takes longer to cook than Maine lobster). After 12 minutes, immediately plunge the lobster into ice water. Remove the tail meat and slice into 5 pieces.

3. Cut decorative stars into the shiitake mushroom caps and grill until tender.

4. Mound the salad greens on a chilled plate, place the lobster around the salad, and top with the Garlic Chips and sesame seeds. Toss the shiitake mushrooms in 1 tbsp. of the dressing and place around the lobster. Drizzle 2 tbsp. of dressing over the lobster.

HOUSE SPECIAL ROLL

Wherever I go, this is one item I always like to make, and in fact, it's popular at all my locations. The basic ingredients are tuna, avocado, and chives—the rest I improvise on the spot. I use whatever strikes my fancy, especially the freshest fish of the day. Sushi has to hold together, but you shouldn't roll it or squeeze it too tight. Nothing worse than hard sushi! It must be firm enough to be picked up with your fingers, yet come apart light and fluffy in the mouth. The rice should merge with the fish, becoming more and more delicious with each bite—that's the ideal. —*N.M.*

MAKES 6 PIECES

1 sheet dried *nori*, 4 in. (10 cm) by 7½ in. (19 cm)
  (If using *sushi nori*, simply cut a sheet in half and you
  will have two sheets of this size)
1 cup (130 g) Vinegared Sushi Rice (*shari*) (p. 185)
Grated wasabi to taste

½ oz. (15 g) fresh tuna
½ oz. (15 g) smoked salmon
½ oz. (15 g) white fish, such as fluke
½ oz. (15 g) *hamachi* yellowtail
10 chives, cut into 4 in. (10 cm) lengths
½ avocado
1 tbsp. *tobiko* flying fish roe
1 paper-thin daikon peel, 4 in. (10 cm) by 7½ in. (19 cm)

1. Cut each fish into strips, ½ in. (1 cm) thick by 4 in. (10 cm) long. Cut the avocado into thin strips.

2. Place the nori sheet flat, shiny side down and shorter side across. (Place the nori sheet on a bamboo mat if available, as this will prevent nori from getting wet.) Moisten your hands with "te-zu" (a mixture of 1 part vinegar and 3 parts water in a small bowl) to prevent the rice from sticking to your hands.

3. Leaving ½ in. (1 cm) of the nori sheet free on the side nearest you and 2 in. (5 cm) free on the far side, spread out the Vinegared Sushi Rice evenly, using your free hand to prevent rice overflowing at the sides.

4. With your fingers, make a shallow trough from right to left in the center of rice, for even rolling after putting in the ingredients.

5. Using your index finger, apply the wasabi in a single motion along the trough from right to left, then place one line of strips of each kind of fish (4 layers in all), followed by the chives and avocado. Top with flying fish roe.

6. You do not roll the nori but fold it: Lift the end of the nori nearest you and carefully fold it over the filling, with a rolling motion, to let the side of the nori sheet nearest you meet the far edge of the sheet. Lightly press down as you go, as this makes an even cylinder. Unwrap the bamboo mat, if using.

7. Roll the daikon peel around the entire roll.

8. Place the roll on a cutting board, seam-side down. Cut in half crosswise, then cut each half into 3 equal pieces.

DESSERTS

BANANA HARUMAKI WITH SESAME ICE CREAM

The key in this Nobu Miami signature dish has got to be the *dulce de leche*, a sweet dairy paste that is a daily staple throughout South America. They spread it on bread and crackers as well as using it to prepare desserts. Very easy to make, you just boil condensed milk unopened in the can until it caramelizes to a rich brown. The consistency depends on how long you cook it, but five hours for a 14-ounce can is about right for our Banana Harumaki. Remember that the heat from deep-frying the spring roll wrapper will make the *dulce de leche* run slightly. —N.M.

SERVES 8 (2 PIECES PER PERSON)

4 fresh bananas, cut into quarters
16 spring roll wrappers (7 in./17 cm square)
16 *shiso* leaves
3 to 4 tbsp. Dulce de Leche (recipe follows)
1 egg yolk, beaten, for sealing the wrappers
Vegetable oil for deep-frying
4 passion fruits
Yuzu Meringues (p. 185)
Sesame Ice Cream (p. 185)

1. Lay a spring roll wrapper on a flat surface and spray with water. Place a shiso leaf, then a banana quarter on the wrapper. Place the Dulce de Leche in a pastry bag and pipe out, from left to right, 2 tsp. to cover the top of the banana. Roll in the wrapper. Brush the egg yolk on the edge of the wrapper and seal. Repeat with the rest of the wrappers.

2. Fry the rolls in 325 °F (160 °C) oil. Transfer to a paper-lined plate to drain any excess oil and allow to cool slightly.

3. Cut each roll in half on an angle. Arrange two halves on individual plates, or arrange all rolls on a platter. Cut the passion fruits in half and squeeze the runny flesh and seeds on top of the rolls.

4. Crumble the Yuzu Meringues in a plastic bag. Sprinkle around the sides of the rolls and top each roll with a scoop of Sesame Ice Cream.

DULCE DE LECHE
MAKES 14 OZ. (400 G)

One 14 oz. (400 g) can sweetened condensed milk

Remove the label from the can and put in a pot. Add enough water to cover the can by at least 4 in. (10 cm), and bring water to a boil over high heat. Lower heat and simmer for 6 hours. Do not forget to add water to keep the level above the can, or the can may burst. Leave the can in the water to cool, then remove from the pot. Leave for 24 hours at room temperature before use.

CHOCOLATE-GLAZED CHERIMOYA MOUSSE BISCUIT

Joel Lahon is our resident master *patissier* at Nobu Miami. He has his own unique creative genius that never fails to excite me. Here he reinvents the *cherimoya* "custard apple," a very popular South American fruit with a light green skin and creamy white flesh that's also a major crop in Andalusia. Joel tops this off with Strawberry Red Bell Pepper Sorbet and Shiso Leaf Crystals—a truly exotic combination that showcases Joel's inventive passion. —*T.B.*

10½ oz. (300 g) milk chocolate, roughly chopped

10½ oz. (300 g) cacao butter, roughly chopped

1 cylinder Cherimoya Mousse in Biscuit Case
(recipe follows)

Chocolate Mat (p. 186)

8 recipes Shiso Leaf Powder (p. 186)

1 recipe Strawberry and Red Pepper Sorbet (p. 186)

8 Shiso Leaf Crystals (p. 186)

1 recipe Strawberry Red Pepper Sauce (p. 186)

1. Unmold the Cherimoya Mousse Biscuit and cut into 8 pieces.

2. Fill a medium saucepan ¼ full with water and bring to a simmer. Place the milk chocolate and cacao butter in a heat-proof bowl and set over the saucepan. Turn off heat, and stir until completely melted. Dip the Cherimoya Mousse Biscuit into the chocolate glaze to coat. Let set at room temperature.

3. Place a Chocolate Mat on a serving plate. Top with a Cherimoya Mousse Biscuit, Shiso Leaf Powder, Strawberry Red Pepper Sorbet and a Shiso Leaf Crystal. Dot with Strawberry Red Pepper Sauce. Repeat with the rest of the biscuits.

CHERIMOYA MOUSSE IN BISCUIT CASES

MAKES 3 LONG CYLINDERS

Equipment

3 long cylinder molds, 1½ in. (3.75 cm) in diameter and 23 in. (58 cm) long for each

1 baking tray, 17 in. (43 cm) by 23 in. (58 cm)

Baking papers

Biscuit Cases

7 oz. (200 g) confectioner's sugar (3½ cups)

4½ oz. (130 g) all-purpose flour (scant 1 cup)

7 oz. (200 g) almond powder (2⅓ cups)

11½ oz. (325 g) whole eggs (6 large eggs)

9 oz. (260 g) egg whites (from 7 to 8 large eggs)

3 oz. (90 g) superfine sugar (scant ½ cup)

6 tbsp. (90 g) butter, melted

Cherimoya Mousse

1 lb. plus 1½ oz. (500 g) cherimoya purée
(from 3 to 4 cherimoyas, seeds removed)

1 tbsp. lemon juice

⅓ oz. (10 g) gelatin sheets, reconstituted in cold water

1¼ cups (300 ml) whipping cream

Italian Meringue (p. 186)

1. Make the Biscuit Cases: Preheat oven to 460 °F (240 °C).

2. In a large bowl, sift together the confectioner's sugar and all-purpose flour. Combine with almond powder. Set aside.

3. Place the whole eggs in the bowl of an electric mixer fitted with the whip attachment, and beat the whole eggs to ribbon consistency (p. 194). Transfer to a small bowl and set aside. Place the egg whites and superfine sugar in the bowl of the electric mixer fitted with the whip attachment, and beat until soft peaks form.

4. Fold the dry ingredients into the beaten whole eggs, then fold in the egg whites and melted butter.

5. Pour the mixture onto a baking sheet and bake until the dough begins to brown, 6 to 8 minutes. Remove from the oven and allow to set at room temperature.

6. Meanwhile, make 3 strips, about 23 in. long by 4.5 in. wide (58 x 11 cm) out of baking paper. When the biscuit sheet is cool enough to handle, cut it lengthwise into 3 strips 3.5 in. (8.75 cm) wide. Place each biscuit strip on top of a baking paper strip, roll, and insert into a cylindrical tube mold. Set aside.

7. Make the Cherimoya Mousse: Purée the cherimoya flesh in a food processor along with the lemon juice.

8. Combine the reconstituted gelatin and half the cherimoya purée in a small saucepan. Place over low heat. Once the temperature reaches 104 °F (40 °C), stir to dissolve the gelatin. Add the remaining half of the cherimoya purée and pass through a sieve. Set aside.

9. In the bowl of an electric mixer with the whip attachment, whip the heavy cream into soft peaks. Cover and refrigerate.

10. Fold the Italian Meringue into the cherimoya mixture. Fold in the whipped cream. Transfer into a pastry bag and pipe into the biscuit cases. Freeze for 24 hours.

FOR AN EASIER OPTION: Bake the biscuit dough in any small mold, in individual portions. When the biscuits are cooled, pipe the Cherimoya Mousse on top. Freeze them for 24 hours before serving.

NOBU "CIGARS" WITH MILK CHOCOLATE MISO MOUSSE

When Joel told me "Hey Nobu, I'm thinking to make something with chocolate and red miso," I could scarcely imagine what an impossibly fine match these two things could be. Miami being so close to Cuba, you see cigar smokers about town. Taking inspiration from their *ambiente*, we fashioned a finger food dessert—the perfect thing to pass around like cigars toward the end of a party. Besides chocolate, we've also created a green tea version and a fruit version. —*N.M.*

12 Chocolate Cigars (recipe follows)
Milk Chocolate Miso Mousse (recipe follows)

Place the Milk Chocolate Miso Mousse into a pastry bag fitted with a small round tip. Fill each Chocolate Cigar with the mousse. Serve in a box like cigars.

CHOCOLATE CIGARS
MAKES 12 CIGAR-SHAPED STICKS

$2^2/_3$ oz. (75 g) all-purpose flour ($^2/_3$ cup)
$1^3/_4$ oz. (50 g) confectioner's sugar ($^1/_3$ cup)
$1^3/_4$ tbsp. (10 g) unsweetened cacao powder
$1^3/_4$ oz. (50 g) unsalted butter, softened (4 tbsp.)
$1^3/_4$ oz. (50 g) beaten egg whites ($1^1/_2$ large egg whites)

12 cannoli molds $^1/_2$ in. (1.25 cm) in diameter

1. Preheat oven to 340 °F (170 °C).

2. Sift together flour, sugar and cacao powder. Transfer, along with the butter, into the bowl of an electric mixer fitted with a paddle attachment. Mix on low speed until incorporated, then slowly add the egg whites. If you have a Pacojet (p. 193), you can simply Process all the ingredients and go on to step 3.

3. Spread in a fine layer on a sheet pan lined with a non-stick silicone mat. Bake until dry to the touch, about 4 minutes.

4. Cut into 4 in. (10 cm) squares while warm and roll each square around a cannoli mold. Allow to set at room temperature. If not using immediately, keep the sticks in an airtight container with a silica gel packet in a cool, dry place.

MILK CHOCOLATE MISO MOUSSE
MAKES 4 CUPS (960 ML)

$2^1/_3$ oz. (65 g) superfine sugar ($5^1/_2$ tbsp.)
1 tbsp. *hatcho* miso (red miso)
2 tsp. rice vinegar
$^1/_2$ cup (120 ml) heavy cream
3 oz. (90 g) beaten egg yolks ($2^1/_2$ large egg yolks)

2 gelatin sheets (4 g), soaked in cold water and squeezed to drain
$^1/_2$ lb. (225 g) milk chocolate, roughly chopped
2 cups (480 ml) whipping cream

1. Place the sugar with 1 tbsp. water in a small saucepan. Heat over low heat, stirring to dissolve, and cook until golden. Quickly mix in the miso and vinegar, then add the heavy cream. When the mixture reaches 176 °F (80 °C), remove from heat. Add the egg yolks and gelatin and mix thoroughly.

2. Place the chopped chocolate in a bowl. Beat the whipping cream until soft peaks form. Strain the miso mixture into the chocolate, stirring with a rubber spatula. Fold in the whipped cream. Pour into a pastry bag and refrigerate for 1 hour.

PINEAPPLE SHAVED ICE WITH EXOTIC SAUCES

Miami is a true paradise for fruit, with everything from oranges, lemons and other citrus to lucuma, cherimoya, pineapples, red papayas and passion fruit from the Caribbean and South America available all year round. How many cities are there in the world where you can head to the beach and enjoy a nice cool shaved ice any time you want? Perfect for parties, where you can let each guest choose their favorite local organic fruit and slice it on the spot for an instant topping. What could be more refreshing at a casual lunch? Drizzle on bright Mora Red Sauce for that sassy tropical touch! —*N.M.*

SERVES 8

Pineapple Shaved Ice
1 fresh extra-sweet pineapple, peeled (½ lb./250 g)
2 cups (480 ml) water
3 tbsp. Simple Syrup (p. 185)

Coconut Sauce
2 fresh coconuts in shell
1 tbsp. Simple Syrup (p. 185)

Mora Red Sauce
7 oz. (200 g) fresh mora berries
   (any sweet berries can be substituted)
⅓ cup (80 ml) Simple Syrup (p. 185)

Toppings
8 fresh lychee, peeled
1 fresh red papaya, peeled and sliced
2 fresh passion fruit, peeled and sliced

1. Make the Pineapple Shaved Ice: Cut the pineapple flesh into chunks and purée in a food processor. Combine with water and Simple Syrup in a stainless-steel container. Keep in a freezer for 24 hours.

2. Make the Coconut Sauce: Remove some of the brown fibers from the outer skin of the coconuts and find the dimples. Insert a small knife into a dimple and make a hole. Pour the coconut juice out into a bowl and reserve. Cut open the coconuts and scrape out the white flesh. Place the juice, flesh and Simple Syrup in a food processor and pulse into a purée. Strain through a fine-mesh sieve and refrigerate.

3. Make the Mora Red Sauce: Combine the mora flesh and Simple Syrup in a food processor and pulse into a purée. Strain through a fine-mesh sieve and refrigerate.

4. Shave the frozen pineapple purée with an ice shaving machine. (Alternatively, shave with a mandoline or fork.) Put the shavings in a glass, top with the fresh fruits and spoon the sauces over.

LUCUMA, CHOCOLATE, ESPRESSO AND BANANA

A diverse tableau of flavors and textures such as only Joel can conceive, featuring the star of Peruvian fruit, the lucuma, with an intriguing taste somewhere between a chestnut and a persimmon. Joel uses it three ways here: as a foam, a sauce and a powder. The lines drawn on the plate are Lucuma Powder and Lucuma Sauce. From front to back in the photo are Banana Mousse on Chocolate Sauce, a dot of Lucuma Sauce, Espresso Ice Cream on a Chocolate Brownie with Chocolate Croquant, Lucuma Foam and, furthest back, a square of dark chocolate. Note the perfect balance of volume and form between all the various elements. —*N.M.*

Starting from the front of the picture:
Lucuma Powder (p. 187)
Chocolate Sauce (p. 187)
Banana Mousse (p. 187)
Lucuma Sauce (p. 187)
Chocolate Brownie (recipe follows)
Espresso Ice Cream (recipe follows)
Chocolate Croquant (p. 187)
Lucuma Foam Base (p. 187)
8 squares gourmet dark chocolate

1. Sprinkle a line of the Lucuma Powder on each serving plate. Using the photo as a guide, pipe out a line of Lucuma Sauce across the powder. Where they cross, pipe out the Chocolate Sauce and flatten a little with a palette knife. Leave until the chocolate becomes firm.

2. Unmold the Banana Mousse and cut into 16 pieces. (You will only need 8 pieces.)

3. Using the photo as a guide, place a piece of Banana Mousse on top of the chocolate. Dot with the Lucuma Sauce. Arrange the Chocolate Brownie, Espresso Ice Cream, and Chocolate Croquant.

4. Shake the stored Lucuma Foam Base well. Pour into a siphon (p. 194). Set 2 chargers according to the manufacturer's instructions. Make a mound of form on the plate.

5. Add the Espresso Ice Cream on the side. Repeat for the remaining servings.

CHOCOLATE BROWNIES

MAKES 16 SMALL BROWNIES

A metal cake pan, 10 in. (25 cm) square and 1 in. (2.5 cm) deep

9 oz. (250 g) chocolate (85% cacao), roughly chopped
5⅓ oz. (150 g) unsalted butter (10½ tbsp.)
9 oz. (250 g) beaten eggs (5 large eggs)
5⅓ oz. (150 g) superfine sugar (¾ cup)

2 oz. (60 g) rice flour (generous ⅓ cup)
Butter and flour for greasing a cake pan
1 biscuit sheet (see p. 168 for Biscuit Case recipe), cut to fit into the cake pan

1. Preheat oven to 340 °F (170 °C).

2. Place the chocolate and butter in a metal bowl and set it over a saucepan of hot water over very low heat. Melt the chocolate and butter, stirring, until smooth and shiny.

3. Place the eggs in a bowl and add the sugar and rice flour. Fold in the chocolate mixture. Place the biscuit sheet in a greased, floured cake pan. Pour the batter on top and bake for 10 to 15 minutes, or until the center of the brownie is still a bit soft. Allow to cool in the pan and cut into 16 squares. (You will only need 8 pieces.)

ESPRESSO ICE CREAM

MAKES 5 CUPS (1.2 L)

5⅓ oz. (150 g) egg yolks (from 7 large eggs)
8 oz. (225 g) superfine sugar (1 cup plus 2 tbsp.)
19⅓ oz. (550 g) whole milk (2¼ cups)
12⅓ oz. (350 g) heavy cream (1½ cups)

5 tbsp. freshly brewed espresso
1 tbsp. coffee extract
⅙ cup (40 ml) single malt whisky

1. Whisk the egg yolks and sugar in a medium bowl. Set aside. Combine the milk and cream in a saucepan and heat until warm. Pour the egg yolk mixture into the pan over low heat, stirring continuously until the liquid reaches 176 °F (80 °C). Strain through a fine-mesh sieve into a bowl. Stir in the espresso, coffee extract and whisky.

2. Place the bowl over an ice bath, stirring from time to time. When cool, remove from the ice bath. The mixture ideally should be refrigerated for 4 hours.

3. Process in an ice cream machine according to the manufacturer's instructions. Pack into containers and freeze overnight.

GUAVA SPOON

Ferran Adrià of El Bulli has popularized many techniques throughout the culinary world, and his "Reverse Spherication" method, which uses sodium alginate and calcium chloride to surround a flavorful filling with a soft skin, has become a standard in many restaurants. Here we take the pulp of a *guayaba*—that Caribbean and South American tropical fruit that everyone should know as "guava"—and use Adrià's technique to shape it into a tablespoon-size ball that turns liquid in your mouth as the coating dissolves. A surprising and refreshing party treat. —*T.B.*

Guava Mixture
½ lb. (225 g) guava pulp (1⅓ cups)
2 tbsp. Simple Syrup (p. 185)
2 tsp. (6 g) calcium chloride

Sodium Alginate Bath
1 qt. (1 L) cold water
2 tsp. (5 g) sodium alginate powder

About 1 qt. (1 L) warm water
About 1 qt. (1 L) Simple Syrup (p. 185)

1. In a blender, mix the fresh guava purée, Simple Syrup and calcium chloride. Transfer to a bowl and place in the refrigerator for 24 hours to release the air bubbles from the mixture.

2. Mix 1 qt. (1 L) cold water and sodium alginate powder in a blender. Transfer to a shallow, wide container about 12 in. long by 6 in. wide, 2.5 in. deep (30 x 15 x 5 cm). Refrigerate for 1 hour. Have ready warm water and the Simple Syrup in separate containers. (Shallow, wide containers like the one used for the sodium alginate bath work well.)

3. Use a soup spoon to scoop the guava mixture. Briefly tip the spoon into the sodium alginate bath, then remove the spoon quickly, leaving the guava mixture to set for about 3 minutes. Use a second spoon to move the sphere to the warm water bath for about 3 minutes, then transfer it to the Simple Syrup. Repeat with the rest of the guava mixture. If you make multiple balls at once, do not let them touch in the sodium alginate bath, or they will stick together.

4. Serve each guava ball on a serving spoon.

ALFAJORES

Alfajores are a kind of South American macaroon, very popular in Peru, typically made with *dulce de leche* and jam sandwiched between layers of shortbread—though every family and shop has its own variation. Our version is rolled, and the *dulce de leche* is coated with flaked coconut. Originally *alfajores* were Middle Eastern sweets (hence the Arabic "*al*"), which traveled to medieval Andalusia and from there to South America. In Spain, they are eaten mainly at Christmas, but they make perfect little one-bite treats for any festive occasion. —*T.B.*

MAKES 15 COOKIES

Shortbread Rounds

¾ cup (150 g) superfine sugar

1 stick plus 2 tbsp. (5¼ oz./150 g) unsalted butter, softened

½ tsp. salt

2 oz. (60 g) beaten egg yolks, (from 3½ large eggs)

2½ oz. (70 g) almond powder (¾ cup)

7 oz. (200 g) cake flour (1½ cups)

1½ tbsp. (20 g) baking powder

Additional Ingredients

Dulce de Leche (p. 166)

3 tbsp. coconut shreds

1. In a large bowl, sift together the almond powder, cake flour and baking powder. Set aside.

2. Place the butter, sugar and salt in the bowl of an electric mixer fitted with the paddle attachment, and beat on medium speed until the mixture is creamy and pale in color. Beat in the egg yolks for 30 seconds.

3. Reduce speed to low, and gradually add the flour mixture to get a smooth paste. Mix for 30 seconds. Cover the bowl with plastic wrap and refrigerate for 1 hour.

4. Dust work surface with flour. Gently roll out the dough to ⅓ in. thick. Cut into 30 small rounds with a ring mold. (A mold 1½ in./3.75 cm in diameter was used for the cookies in the photo.) Cover with plastic wrap and refrigerate.

5. Heat oven to 360 °F (180 °C). Place the rounds on a baking sheet lined with parchment paper and bake until pale golden, about 4 to 5 minutes. Cool on a wire rack.

6. Put the Dulce de Leche into a pastry bag with a small round tip. Pipe onto a shortbread round and sandwich with another shortbread round. Spread the dried coconut on a plate and roll the shortbread sandwiches in the coconut to coat the edges.

MIAMI BENTO BOX

Undoubtedly the "king of kings" among Nobu desserts, this Bento Box comes in several variations that Joel has devised. Fondant chocolate is a specialty of his native France, so we let him do his thing. Fork into the green tea cake and out pours a river of chocolate sauce. And what flavor do you think the ice cream is? Burnt sugar caramel with a tiny drop of soy sauce. The rice puffs are also labor intensive, but all that uncompromising effort really shows in the taste. —*N.M.*

SERVES 8 TO 10

8 parchment squares, each 4 in. (10 cm) square

8 ring molds, 2¾ in. (7 cm) in diameter and 1¾ in. (4.5 cm) high for each

Fondant Chocolate
1 recipe Green Tea Mix (recipe follows)
1 recipe Dark Chocolate Mix (p. 182)

Unsalted butter, softened
Non-stick cooking spray
Soy Caramel Ice Cream (p. 182)
Cinnamon Rice Puffs (p. 182)
Fresh fruits, such as star fruit, longan, and raspberry

1. Preheat an oven to 360 °F (180 °C).

2. Place the parchment squares on a sheet pan. Butter the inside of each ring mold and place on top of the parchment squares. Spray vegetable oil onto the parchment paper inside the ring molds.

3. Pipe the Green Tea Mix into each ring mold, filling each ⅓ full. Pipe an equal volume of Dark Chocolate Mix into each mold, inserting the piping tip below the surface of the green tea mixture. The chocolate mixture will push the green tea mixture up and form a ball inside. The chocolate mixture should not be visible, and the green tea mixture should now come ⅔ up the side of the ring mold. Top each with Green Tea Mix to cover the Dark Chocolate Mix, as needed.

4. Bake until dry on the outside but still runny inside, 10 to 12 minutes. Immediately remove from the oven and rest at room temperature for a few minutes. Unmold with an offset spatula and place in a bento box.

5. Serve with a scoop of Soy Caramel Ice Cream on Cinnamon Rice Puffs and garnish with fresh fruit.

GREEN TEA MIX
MAKES ENOUGH FOR 8 TO 10 MOLDS

6 tbsp. (60 g) rice flour
2 tbsp. (20 g) green tea powder
10 large whole eggs, beaten
7 oz. (200 g) superfine sugar (scant 1 cups)
17⅔ oz. (500 g) white chocolate, roughly chopped
17⅔ oz. (500 g) unsalted butter, cut into pieces (4 sticks plus 3 tbsp.)

1. Sift together the rice flour and green tea powder into a bowl.

2. Combine the whole eggs and superfine sugar in the bowl of an electric mixer fitted with a whip attachment, and beat until they fall from the beater in a ribbon.

3. Place the white chocolate and butter in a heat-proof bowl and set it over a saucepan of hot water on low heat. Melt the chocolate and butter, stirring, until smooth and shiny. Set aside.

4. With the electric mixer on low, gradually add the flour mixture to the eggs and mix for 1 minute. Add the chocolate mixture and mix at medium speed for 1 minute. Pour into a pastry bag and use immediately.

DARK CHOCOLATE MIX

6 tbsp. (62 g) rice flour

10 large whole eggs, beaten

7 oz. (200 g) superfine sugar (scant 1 cup)

17⅔ oz. (500 g) dark chocolate, (70% cacao), roughly chopped

17⅔ oz. (500 g) unsalted butter (4 sticks plus 3 tbsp.), cut into pieces

1. Sift the rice flour into a bowl.

2. Combine the whole eggs and superfine sugar in the bowl of an electric mixer fitted with a whip attachment, and beat until they fall from the beater in a ribbon.

3. Place the dark chocolate and butter in a heat-proof bowl and set it over a saucepan of hot water over low heat. Melt the chocolate and butter, stirring, until smooth and shiny. Set aside.

4. With the electric mixer on low, gradually add the rice flour to the egg mixture and mix for 1 minute. Add the chocolate mixture and mix at medium speed for 1 minute. Pour into a pastry bag and use immediately.

SOY CARAMEL ICE CREAM

4½ oz. (130 g) superfine sugar (½ cup plus 1 tbsp.)

2 tbsp. heavy cream

2 oz. (55 g) melted unsalted butter (3¾ tbsp.)

1½ tsp. low-sodium soy sauce

1 tsp. rice vinegar

20 oz. (570 g) whole milk (2 cups plus 6 tbsp.)

2¾ oz. (80 g) large beaten egg yolks (4 medium eggs)

Scant ½ cup (50 g) milk powder

Heaping 2 tbsp. (30 g) glucose powder

1. In a small saucepan, heat the superfine sugar until golden brown, being careful not to burn. Add the soy sauce, vinegar, butter and heavy cream.

2. Add the whole milk and mix thoroughly until incorporated. Add the egg yolks, milk powder and glucose powder. Heat until the temperature reaches at 176 °F (80 °C), then strain through a fine mesh sieve into a bowl.

3. Place the bowl over an ice bath to cool, stirring from time to time. The mixture ideally should be refrigerated for 4 hours before processing.

4. Process in an ice cream machine according to the manufacturer's instructions. Pack into containers and freeze overnight.

CINNAMON RICE PUFFS

½ cup (90 g) dry white rice

1 qt. (1 L) water

2 tbsp. confectioner's sugar

1 tsp. ground cinnamon

Vegetable oil for deep-frying

1. In a heavy medium-sized pan mix the rice with the water. Bring to boil, cover and lower the heat. Gently simmer for 25 to 30 minutes.

2. Strain through a fine-mesh sieve. Spread the rice out grain by grain on a sheet pan lined with baking paper, and dry for 12 hours in a 86 °F (35 °C) oven.

3. Deep-fry in the oil at 392 °F (200 °C) until the rice is puffed, about 10 seconds. Transfer the rice to a paper-lined tray to drain excess oil. Combine the confectioner's sugar with the cinnamon and dust over the rice puffs while hot. Toss to coat. Store the rice in an airtight container with a silica gel packet in a cool, dry place.

ADDITIONAL RECIPES

pp. 18, 144
MOMIJI OROSHI

Peel a daikon. Grate and lightly drain in a fine-mesh sieve. For every tablespoon of grated daikon, mix in ½ teaspoon of red chili paste.

p. 36
WHITE PONZU
MAKES SCANT 1 CUP (200 ML)

4 tbsp. white soy sauce
8 tbsp. rice vinegar
2 tbsp. lemon juice
1 piece dried *kombu*, ¼ in. (5 mm) square

Combine all ingredients and refrigerate overnight (at least 8 hours).

pp. 42, 59, 82, 134, 161
GARLIC CHIPS
MAKES 1 CUP (210 ML)

10 cloves garlic, thinly sliced on a mandoline
1 cup (240 ml) whole milk
3 cups (720 ml) canola oil

1. Preheat the oil to 300 °F (150 °C).

2. Place the garlic and milk in a saucepan and bring to a boil to remove bitterness. After a few seconds, remove the garlic. Wash in cold water and pat dry.

3. Deep-fry the garlic slices in the oil over low heat. When they turn light golden, transfer immediately to a paper-lined dish (they will continue to cook).

p. 52
YUZU MOJO
MAKES 2⅔ CUPS (630 ML)

1 cup (240 ml) extra-virgin olive oil
2 cloves garlic, peeled and finely sliced
½ tsp. cumin seeds, toasted
2 tsp. salt (or more)
2 tsp. black peppercorns, toasted and ground
1 large white onion, finely chopped

1 cup (240 ml) sour orange juice (p. 195)
½ cup (120 ml) *yuzu* juice
1 tbsp. soy sauce
2 tsp. chopped fresh oregano (or ½ tsp. dried oregano)

1. Heat the oil to medium-hot, but not smoking.

2. Meanwhile, place the garlic, cumin, salt and peppercorns in a food processor or mortar and grind to a semi-fine paste. Transfer to a heat-proof bowl and add the onion. Pour the hot oil over, being careful not to burn yourself, and allow to cool for 20 minutes.

3. Whisk in the orange and yuzu juices, soy sauce and oregano. Add salt to taste. Keeps refrigerated for 3 to 4 days.

pp. 57, 73, 76, 98, 132
DASHI STOCK
MAKES 2 CUPS (480 ML)

1 piece dried *kombu*, 2 in. (5 cm) square
2¼ cups (500 ml) water
1 cup (15 g) dried bonito flakes

1. Soak the kombu in the water overnight. Take out the kombu and bring the water to a boil. (Alternatively, combine the kombu and water in a pot over medium-low heat. Just before the water boils, take out the kombu.)

2. Add the bonito flakes and turn off the heat. Leave undisturbed until the bonito flakes sink to the bottom of the pan, then strain through a fine-mesh sieve lined with a paper towel.

p. 60
AMAZU
MAKES ABOUT ¾ CUP (180 ML)

½ cup (120 ml) rice vinegar
6 tbsp. granulated sugar
2½ tsp. sea salt

Heat the rice vinegar, sugar and salt in a small saucepan over medium heat. Stir, and when the sugar has dissolved, immediately remove from heat. Allow to cool to room temperature.

p. 60
ROCOTO MUSTARD MISO
MAKES 2½ CUPS (600 ML)

5 tsp. mustard powder
10 tsp. hot water
2 cups + 2 tbsp. (600 g) Nobu-style Saikyo Miso (p. 42)
⅓ cup (75 ml) rice vinegar
½ tbsp. *ají rocoto* paste
2 tsp. roasted sesame oil

In a small cup, mix the mustard powder with the hot water to form a paste. Combine the Nobu-style Saikyo Miso, rice vinegar, ají rocoto paste and sesame oil in a bowl. Mix in the mustard paste.

p. 82
YUZU PONZU
MAKES SCANT 1 CUP (210 ML)

¼ cup (60 ml) soy sauce
½ cup (120 ml) rice vinegar
2 tbsp. *yuzu* juice
1 piece *kombu*, ¾ in. (2 cm) square

Combine all ingredients in a container and refrigerate overnight (or at least 8 hours).

pp. 90, 91, 97, 100, 118, 161
TEMPURA BATTER
MAKES 1½ CUPS (360 ML)

1 large egg yolk
Scant 1 cup (200 ml) ice water
¾ cup (100 g) all-purpose flour

Combine the egg yolk and ice water and mix well. Stir in the flour until barely mixed, ignoring lumps. The batter should not be whisked or the gluten will develop, making the finished tempura chewy and heavy.

pp. 95, 142
COOKED RICE
MAKES 2⅓ CUPS (440 G)

1 cup (200 g) short-grain rice
1 cup plus 3 tbsp. (285 ml) water

1. Place the rice in a bowl and wash gently in several changes of cold water, until the water remains mostly clear. Strain the rice and let it rest for 20 minutes.

2. Combine the rice and water in a heavy saucepan over high heat. Cover with a heavy lid and bring to a boil.

3. Turn the heat to low and continue to cook for 10 to 12 minutes.

4. Turn off the heat and let the rice stand, without opening the lid, for 15 minutes.

5. Remove the lid, being careful not to drip water onto the rice. Gently fold the rice with a spatula from bottom to top to release the steam.

p. 115
SHISO CHIMICHURRI
MAKES 1¾ CUPS (420 M)

Juice of 1½ lemons
1 tbsp. red rice vinegar
10 *shiso* leaves, chopped
1 tbsp. chopped *huacatay* black mint
1 tbsp. garlic purée
1 cup (60 g) chopped parsley
½ cup (120 ml) olive oil
1 tsp. soy sauce
½ tsp. freshly ground black pepper

1. Mix the vinegar and lemon juice. Set aside.

2. Place the garlic, shiso, huacatay and parsley in a blender. Slowly add the oil in a thin stream while blending at low speed.

p. 115
RED ANTICUCHO SAUCE
MAKES 1¼ CUPS (300 ML)

6 tbsp. *ají panca* paste

5 tbsp. Hokusetsu sake
3⅓ tbsp. rice vinegar
2½ tbsp. garlic purée
2 tsp. salt
1 tsp. cumin seeds, toasted and ground
¼ tsp. dried oregano, lightly crushed
3 tbsp. grapeseed oil

Combine all ingredients except oil. Slowly add the oil, whisking constantly to emulsify.

p. 144
SHALLOT TOSAZU
MAKES SCANT 1 CUP (210 ML)

3 shallots, finely chopped
1 tsp. freshly ground black pepper
½ cup (120 ml) Tosazu (p. 105)
5 tbsp. Amazu (p. 183)

Combine all ingredients.

p. 144
MACADAMIA SAUCE
MAKES ABOUT ½ CUP (120 ML)

½ cup (70 g) whole macadamia nuts, roasted until golden brown
1 tbsp. grapeseed oil
1½ tsp. light soy sauce
1 tsp. granulated sugar
1 tsp. *mirin*
½ tsp. rice vinegar
3 tbsp. Dashi Stock (p. 183)
1 tsp. sake

Place the roasted nuts and oil in a blender and mix on high speed to a smooth paste. Transfer to a bowl, add the rest of the ingredients and combine well.

NOTE: Pine nuts, cashews, almonds or hazelnuts can also be used.

p. 146
VEAL STOCK
MAKES ABOUT 1 QT. (1 L)

2 lbs. (900 g) veal bones
1.8 qt (1.7 L) water

1 medium carrot, cut into chunks
1 medium onion, cut into chunks
1 medium leek, tender part, cut into chunks
1 tsp. tomato paste

Bouquet Garni
½ tsp. peppercorns
1 sprig thyme
1 sprig parsley
1 bay leaf

1. Place the veal bones in a single layer in a roasting pan. Roast about 40 minutes at 400 °F (200 °C) until nicely browned. Being careful not to burn your hands, remove from the oven and add the tomato paste. Stir. Return to the oven and cook 10 minutes more.

2. Transfer the veal bones to a large stock pot. Cover with the water. Bring to a gentle simmer and cook for 12 hours.

3. Meanwhile, roast the vegetable at 400 °F (200 °C) until the edges are browned. To make the Bouquet Garni, wrap the peppercorns, thyme, parsley and bay leaf in a piece of cheesecloth and tie with string. Add the vegetables to the simmering water, along with the wrapped herbs, and cook for 2 more hours.

4. Strain the stock through a sieve lined with cheesecloth. Return to the pot and place over medium heat. Pour the stock into a smaller size pot as it is reduced. Bring to a gentle simmer and reduce by half, skimming off any scum that forms.

p. 146
AKA DEN MISO
MAKES ABOUT 2 CUPS (480 ML)

⅓ cup (90 g) *hatcho* miso
½ cup (100 g) granulated sugar
½ cup plus 2 tbsp. (150 ml) sake
½ cup plus 2 tbsp. (150 ml) *mirin*

Combine sake, mirin and sugar in a metal bowl and slowly add the miso, mixing with a hand blender. Bring water to a gentle simmer in a saucepan and place the bowl over the pan. Cook, stirring from time to time to evaporate the alcohol, for about 40 minutes.

pp. 146, 172, 176
SIMPLE SYRUP

Place 2 parts of granulated sugar and 1 part water in a saucepan. Bring to a boil and dissolve completely. Remove the pan from heat and allow to cool completely.

p. 146
MANGO SALSA
MAKES 2 CUPS (480 ML)

2 ripe mangoes
1 Japanese cucumber
½ red onion
1 jalapeño
2 tbsp. chopped cilantro
Juice of 2 limes
1 tsp. salt
2 tsp. long pepper, toasted and coarsely ground

Cut the mangoes and cucumber into ¼ in. (6 mm) dice. Cut the red onion into ⅛ in. (3 mm) dice. Mince the jalapeño finely. Combine all the ingredients.

p. 160
CHILI GARLIC SAUCE
MAKES ABOUT 1⅓ CUPS (310 ML)

12 oz. (340 g) Fresno chilis (or jalapeño and habañero)
12 cloves garlic
2 tsp. salt
3 tbsp. sugar
3 tbsp. rice vinegar
1 tbsp. *mirin*

1. Place all ingredients in a food processor and pulse to a coarse paste.

2. Place in a saucepan over medium-high heat and cook about 4 minutes. Bring

to a gentle simmer and continue to cook for 6 more minutes, stirring the bottom so as not to scorch. (The liquid should be almost gone.) Cool to room temperature.

p. 162
VINEGARED SUSHI RICE [*SHARI*]
MAKES ABOUT 7⅓ CUPS (920 G)

2 cups (400 g) short-grain rice
2 cups (480 ml) water

Vinegar Mixture
Scant ½ cup (100 ml) red rice vinegar
1 tbsp. plus 1 tsp. sea salt
½ tbsp. *mirin*
5 tbsp. granulated sugar
1 piece dried *kombu*, 1 in. (2.5 cm) square

1. Make the Vinegar Mixture: Combine 5 tbsp. of the vinegar, sea salt, mirin and sugar in a small saucepan over medium high heat and warm to dissolve the sugar. Add the kombu and remove from heat. When cool, add the rest of vinegar (heating tends to destroy its bouquet). This will yield a scant ⅔ cup (150 ml) of vinegar mixture, which is the minimum possible yield, but use only 5 tbsp. for this recipe. Keep at room temperature.

2. Wash the rice, stirring gently by hand with a circular motion in several changes of cold water until the water remains almost clear. Drain in a sieve.

3. In a heavy pot, combine the rice and water and bring to a boil over high heat.

4. Turn heat down to low, then continue to cook for 10 to 15 minutes. At very end, turn the heat to high for 10 seconds. Remove from heat and let the rice stand for 15 minutes so it steams evenly.

5. Transfer the hot rice to a large bowl, or preferably a wooden sushi tub (*handai*), and sprinkle the vinegar mixture over the rice. Mix the rice with a spatula

or rice paddle, using an angle-slicing motion to combine the rice and vinegar evenly. Do not stir. Allow to cool to body temperature and use immediately.

p. 166
YUZU MERINGUES
MAKES 20 MERINGUES

3 oz. (90 g) egg whites (from 2 to 3 large eggs)
3 oz. (90 g) superfine sugar (scant ½ cup)
2 tbsp. powdered dried *yuzu* peel
3 oz. (90 g) confectioner's sugar (1½ cups)

1. Combine the egg whites and superfine sugar in the bowl of an electric mixer. Use the whisk attachment to whip until the meringue forms stiff peaks.

2. Using a rubber spatula, gradually fold the confectioner's sugar and dried yuzu peel into the meringue.

3. Heat oven to 140 °F (60 °C). Place the meringue in a pastry bag fitted with a medium round tip. Line a sheet pan with a nonstick silicone baking mat. Pipe the meringue, forming domes 1 in. (2.5 cm) in diameter, and bake in the oven until completely dry to the touch but not browned, about 8 hours. If not using immediately, they should be stored in an air-tight container with a silica gel packet in a cool place.

p. 166
SESAME ICE CREAM
MAKES 6 CUPS (900 G)

1 cup (240 ml) whole milk
1 cup (240 ml) heavy cream
3½ oz. (100 g) egg yolks (about 5 large eggs)
3½ oz. (100 g) superfine sugar (½ cup)
1⅓ tsp. (5 g) glucose powder
3 tbsp. (50 g) white sesame paste

1. Combine the milk and heavy cream in a medium saucepan and heat until tepid. Whisk the egg yolks, sugar, and

glucose powder together in a medium bowl. Slowly add the egg mixture to the pan, stirring constantly, and cook until the mixture thickens enough to coat the back of a spoon (180 °F/82 °C). Strain through a fine-mesh sieve into a metal container. Add the sesame paste.

2. Place the container in an ice bath and stir from time to time. When cooled, cover and refrigerate the container for a minimum of 4 hours. (You must cool down the mixture immediately to avoid the development of bacteria, and the refrigeration time stabilizes the ice cream and allows its flavors to mature.)

3. Process in an ice cream machine according to the manufacturer's instructions. Pack into containers and freeze overnight before using.

p. 168
CHOCOLATE MAT
MAKES A HALF SHEET PAN

1 cup (240 ml) water
5¼ oz. (150 g) granulated sugar (¾ cup)
⅞ oz. (25 g) unsweetened cocoa powder (5 tbsp.)
1 tsp. (4 g) agar-agar powder

1. Mix all ingredients in a small saucepan, bring to a boil and cook for 1 minute. Strain through a fine-mesh sieve. Pour the mixture into a half sheet pan lined with plastic wrap. Allow to cool in a refrigerator until firm.

2. Cut into 8 squares of any size (here the mat is cut into 4 in./10 cm squares).

p. 168
SHISO LEAF POWDER
MAKES ABOUT 1 TBSP.

Place 10 Shiso Leaf Crystals (recipe above) in a food processor and pulse into powder. Store in an airtight container with a silica gel packet in a cool, dry place.

p. 168
STRAWBERRY RED PEPPER SORBET
MAKES 4 CUPS

10½ oz. (300 g) red bell peppers (4 small peppers)
10½ oz. (300 g) hulled fresh strawberries, cut into pieces (3 cups whole strawberries)
½ cup plus 4 tsp. (140 ml) water
6½ oz. (180 g) superfine sugar (¾ cup)
2¾ oz. (80 g) glucose powder (⅓ cup)

1. Roast the red bell pepper, turning occasionally, until slightly browned. Plunge in ice water. Peel and remove the seeds. Combine with the fresh strawberries in a food processor and pulse into purée. Pass through a sieve into a non-reactive bowl.

2. In a saucepan, bring the water, superfine sugar and glucose powder to a boil and dissolve thoroughly. Pour the liquid into the red pepper and strawberry mixture. Place the bowl over an ice bath, stirring from time to time. When cool, remove from the ice bath. The mixture should be refrigerated for 4 hours before processing.

3. Process in an ice cream machine according to the manufacturer's instructions. Pack into a container and freeze overnight.

p. 168
SHISO LEAF CRYSTALS
MAKES 20 CRYSTALS

20 *shiso* leaves
¾ cup plus 4 tsp. (200 ml) water
7 oz. (200 g) superfine sugar (1 cup)

1. Preheat oven to 140 °F (60 °C).

2. Bring plenty of water to a boil and blanch the shiso leaves for a few seconds. Shock in ice water and blot dry well.

3. Combine the water and sugar in a saucepan and bring to a boil for 30 seconds. Stir to dissolve the sugar thoroughly. Remove from heat and submerge the shiso leaves in the syrup for 1 hour.

4. Transfer the shiso leaves to a non-stick silicone baking mat and place in the oven. Slowly dry the leaves until the sugar crystallizes, about 8 hours. Store them in an airtight container with a silica gel packet in a cool, dry place.

p. 168
STRAWBERRY RED PEPPER SAUCE

1 small red bell pepper
4 medium-sized fresh strawberries, hulled
1 tsp. superfine sugar

Roast the red bell pepper until slightly browned. Plunge in ice water. Peel and remove the seeds. Combine with the fresh strawberries in a food processor and pulse to purée. Pass through a sieve and transfer to a squeeze bottle.

pp. 168, 187
ITALIAN MERINGUE

3 large egg whites (100 g)
¼ cup (50 g) superfine sugar
1 tsp. water

1. Whip the egg whites to medium peaks in the bowl of an electric mixer fitted with the whip attachment.

2. Combine the water and sugar in a saucepan over medium heat and stir to dissolve. Continue cooking, without stirring, until a candy thermometer reads 244 °F (118 °C), or the syrup reaches the soft ball stage (see p. 194).

3. Remove from heat and add the sugar mixture to the meringue in a thin strip while whipping on medium speed. Beat until stiff peaks foam.

p. 174

LUCUMA POWDER

4 ripe lucuma, peeled and pitted
¾ cup (180 ml) Simple Syrup (p. 185)

1. Preheat the oven to 176 °F (80 °C). Place the lucuma flesh and Simple Syrup in a food processor and pulse into purée. Spread the purée in a very fine layer on top of a non-stick silicone mat and dry in oven for 10 hours.

2. Transfer the dried purée to a food processor and pulse into powder. Keep in an airtight container with a silica gel packet in a cool, dry place.

p. 174

CHOCOLATE SAUCE

MAKES ABOUT 6 TBSP.

3⅓ tbsp. (45 g) superfine sugar
3⅓ tbsp. (50 g) water
3⅓ tbsp. (18 g) cacao powder
1 sheet gelatin (2 g)

Combine the sugar and water in a small saucepan and bring to 220 °F (104 °C). Whisk in the cacao powder and strain. Squeeze the gelatin to drain, add to the pan and dissolve thoroughly. Let it cool to room temperature and keep in a squeeze bottle.

p. 174

BANANA MOUSSE

MAKES 1 CYLINDER (16 PIECES)

1 long cylinder mold, 1½ in. (3.75 cm) in diameter and 23 in. (58 cm) long
* You can also use individual molds, as desired.

2 large bananas, peeled
4 sheets gelatin (10 g), soaked in cold water
Italian Meringue (p. 186)
1 cup (240 ml) whipping cream

1. Cut the bananas into chunks and purée in a food processor. Lightly drain the soaked gelatin. Put the gelatin and banana purée in a saucepan and place over low heat, stirring with a rubber spatula, until the gelatin is thoroughly dissolved. Remove from heat and set aside.

2. Use the whip attachment on an electric mixer to whip the heavy cream into soft peaks. Cover and refrigerate.

3. Fold the Italian Meringue into the banana mixture. Fold in the whipped cream. Transfer the mixture into individual molds and freeze for 24 hours.

p. 174

LUCUMA SAUCE

MAKES 1 CUP (240 ML)

7 oz. (200 g) lucuma pulp (about ¾ cup)
3 tbsp. Simple Syrup (p. 185)
1 tbsp. water

Mix all ingredients to a smooth paste in a blender for about 1 minute. Strain. Pour into a pastry bag to be piped out.

p. 174

CHOCOLATE CROQUANT

3 bananas, peeled
½ cup plus 2 tbsp. Simple Syrup (p. 185)
1½ tbsp. cacao powder
½ cup *panko*
5 tbsp. glucose syrup
6 tbsp. plus 2 tsp. water (100 ml)

1. Preheat an oven to 360 °F (180 °C).

2. Combine all the ingredients in a food processor and pulse to a paste. Pour into a small saucepan and heat, stirring continuously, for 10 minutes. (If you have a Thermomix, simply combine all ingredients and heat and mix for 10 minutes, then proceed to step 3.)

3. Transfer the mixture to a pastry bag fitted with a small round tip. Line a sheet pan with a nonstick silicone mat. Pipe 2 lines across the mat by moving the pastry bag back and forth. Transfer the sheet pan to the oven and bake for 4 minutes. Cut and form into desired shapes while still warm.

p. 174

LUCUMA FOAM BASE

MAKES 1⅔ CUPS (400 ML)

Scant 1 cup (100 ml) whole milk
Scant 1 cup (100 ml) heavy cream
2¾ oz. (80 g) superfine sugar (⅓ cup plus 1 tbsp.)
2 sheets gelatin (5 g), soaked in water
7 oz. (200 g) lucuma pulp (about ¾ cup)

Combine the milk, cream and sugar in a saucepan and place over low heat. When warm, lightly squeeze the soaked gelatin to drain and add to the pan. Stir to dissolve thoroughly. Remove from heat and add the lucuma pulp. Strain into a stainless-steel container and refrigerate for 1 hour.

COCKTAIL RECIPES

NOTE: A 2-ounce shot of alcohol is 60 ml.

p. 25
MELBOURNE MULE   SERVE IN A HIGHBALL GLASS

1 kiwi fruit

2 oz. Trinidad 10 cane rum

Dash Angostura bitters

Ginger beer, to top up the drink

Crushed ice to fill the glass

Blood orange peel, as garnish

Ice

Peel the kiwi fruit and cut into small chunks. Place in a highball glass and muddle. Shake the rum, bitters and ice. Pour into a highball glass. Top up with ginger beer and garnish with the blood orange peel.

p. 28
CUCUMBER MARTINI   SERVE IN A MARTINI GLASS

⅛ European cucumber

1 oz. (30 ml) lychee juice

Dash fresh lime juice

2 oz. Nobu *soju* (or other *shochu*)

2 slices cucumber, as garnish

Ice

Peel the ⅛ cucumber, slice lengthwise into quarters, remove seeds and grate. In a cocktail shaker, combine the grated cucumber with lychee juice, fresh lime juice and Nobu soju. Shake with ice and strain into a chilled glass. Add the cucumber slices.

p. 40
PISCO MORA   SERVE IN A HIGHBALL GLASS

¼ cup (40 g) fresh mora berries or blackberries

2 tsp. raw sugar

½ tsp. ground ginger

½ fresh lime

2 oz. Pisco Acholado

Dash Angostura bitters

1 slice blood orange, as garnish

Ice

Muddle the fresh blackberries in a chilled highball glass. In a cocktail shaker, shake the raw sugar, ground ginger, fresh lime, Pisco Acholado, bitters and ice and pour into a highball glass. Garnish with the blood orange slice.

p. 57
STRAWBERRY BLOODY MARY   SERVE IN A SHOT GLASS

1 oz. (30 ml) strawberry purée

1 oz. Açai-infused vodka (Krome)

Dash *ají rocoto* paste

Dash lime juice

1 carrot stick, as garnish

Ice

Shake all ingredients (except the carrot stick) with ice in a cocktail shaker and strain into a chilled shot glass. Garnish with carrot stick.

p. 60
MIAMI MARGARITA   SERVE IN A SNIFTER OR ROCK GLASS

1 fresh passion fruit, peeled and puréed

Dash fresh lime juice

1 oz. (30 ml) Honey Syrup (recipe follows)

½ tsp. *shichimi* spice powder

2 oz. tequila *añejo*

1 cinnamon stick, as garnish

Ice

Shake the all ingredients (except the cinnamon stick) with ice in a cocktail shaker and pour into a chilled snifter or rock glass. Garnish with the cinnamon stick.

Honey Syrup: Combine honey with lemon slices, orange peels, a cinnamon stick and cloves in a container. Leave for at least two days.

p. 63
CHAMPAGNE 95   SERVE IN A MARTINI GLASS

1 oz. (30 ml) fresh pineapple purée

1 oz. peach liqueur

1 oz. orange brandy

Rosé champagne, to top up

Ice

Shake the pineapple purée, peach liqueur and orange brandy with ice in a cocktail shaker. Pour simultaneously with champagne into a glass.

p. 78

SINGLE MALT AND LUCUMA   SERVE IN A LARGE MARTINI GLASS

½ oz. (15 ml) Honey Syrup (recipe p. 188)

2 oz. (60 ml) lucuma purée

2 oz. (60 ml) single-malt whisky (Yamazaki)

1½ oz. (45 ml) fresh grapefruit juice

2 fresh cranberry, as garnish

Ice

Shake all ingredients (except fresh cranberry) with ice in a cocktail shaker and pour into a chilled martini glass. Garnish with the fresh cranberry.

p. 121

BLOOD ORANGE MARTINI   SERVE IN A MARTINI GLASS

2 oz. fresh blood orange juice

1 oz. fresh orange juice

2½ oz. Nobu *soju* (or other *shochu*)

½ oz. Campari

½ tsp. ground ginger

1 mint leaf, as garnish

Ice

Shake all ingredients (except mint) with ice in a cocktail shaker and strain into a chilled martini glass. Garnish with mint leaf.

p. 134

GINGER AND LYCHEE MARTINI   SERVE IN A MARTINI GLASS

1½ oz. (45 ml) Ginger Infused Brandy (recipe follows)

2 oz. (60 ml) Hokusetsu sake

2 oz. (60 ml) lychee syrup (p. 193)

1 fresh lychee, seeded, as garnish

Ice

Shake all ingredients (except fresh lychee) with ice in a cocktail shaker and strain into a chilled martini glass. Garnish with the fresh lychee.

Ginger Infused Brandy: Combine brandy with sliced ginger in a container. Leave for at least two days.

RESTAURANT LISTS

Nobu Miami Beach
1901 Collins Avenue
Miami Beach, FL 33139, USA
Tel: +1 305 695 3232

Nobu Atlantis
Paradise Island, Nassau, Bahamas
Tel: +1 242 363 3000 ext. 65301
(For dinner reservations, dial ext. 65383)

Nobu New York
105 Hudson Street, New York, NY 10013, USA
Tel: +1 212 219 0500

Nobu Next Door
105 Hudson Street, New York, NY 10013, USA
Tel: +1 212 334 4445

Nobu Fifty Seven
40 West 57th Street, New York, NY 10019, USA
Tel: +1 212 757 3000

Nobu Dallas
400 Crescent Court, Dallas, TX 75201, USA
Tel: +1 214 252 7000

Nobu Las Vegas
4455 Paradise Road, Las Vegas, NV 89169, USA
Tel: +1 702 693 5090

Nobu Malibu
3835 Cross Creek Road #18A
Malibu, CA 90265, USA
Tel: +1 310 317 9140

Nobu Los Angeles
903 North La Cienega Boulevard
West Hollywood, CA 90069,USA
Tel: +1 310 657 5711

Nobu Waikiki
2233 Helumoa Road, Honolulu, HI 96815, USA
Tel: +1 808 237 6999

Nobu San Diego
207 Fifth Avenue, San Diego, CA 92101, USA
Tel: +1 619 814 4124

Nobu Melbourne
Crown Melbourne Australia
8 Whiteman Street
Southbank, VIC 3006, Australia
Tel: +61 (0)3 9696 6566

Nobu Tokyo
1F Toranomon Tower Office
4-1-28, Toranomon, Minato-ku
Tokyo 105-0001, Japan
Tel: +81 (0)3 5733 0070

Nobu InterContinental Hong Kong
18 Salisbury Road, Kowloon, Hong Kong
Tel: +852 2721-1211

Nobu Milano
Armani Complex, Via Manzoni 31
20121 Milano, Italy
Tel: +39 02 7231 8645

Nobu @ Badrutt's Palace
Via Serlas 27, CH-7500 St. Moritz, Switzerland
Tel: +41 (0)81-837-1000

Nobu London
19 Old Park Lane, London W1K 1LB, UK
Tel: +44 (0)20 7447 4747

Nobu Berkeley St.
15 Berkeley Street, London W1J 8DY, UK
Tel: +44 (0)20 7290 9222

Matsuhisa Aspen
303 East Main Street, Aspen, CO 81611, USA
Tel: +1 970 544 6628

Matsuhisa Beverly Hills
129 North La Cienega Boulevard
Beverly Hills, CA 90211, USA
Tel: +1 310 659 9639

Ubon by Nobu
34 Westferry Circus, Canary Wharf
London, E14 8RR, UK
Tel: +44 (0)20 7719 7800

 http://www.noburestaurants.com/

GLOSSARY

Agua de chile   A spicy, tart, translucent red liquid, a specialty of Sinaloa in Mexico.

Aioli   Originally a creamy Provençal garlic and oil sauce similar to mayonnaise, but often refers to any mayonnaise-based sauce.

Ají amarillo   A long slim Peruvian pepper, *Capsicum baccatum*, yellowish-green when young, turning to orange when ripe. Medium-hot, with a pleasantly fruity flavor.

Ají limo   A Peruvian variety of the habañero pepper, *Capsicum chinense*. Extremely hot.

Ají panca   A large, mild Peruvian pepper in the *Capsicum annuum* species (which also includes the jalapeño and serrano varieties).

Ají rocoto   A plump, small red Peruvian pepper cultivated for at least 5000 years, *Capsicum pubescens*, meaty and very hot.

Ají rocoto vidrio   see *vidrio*.

Akami tuna loin   Bright red, lean part of tuna meat. As the akami quickly oxidizes, try to prevent it from exposing in the air as possible as you can. See also *toro*.

Amaranth   A weedy cooking green, somewhat like dandelion in flavor, but with brilliant red bunches of tiny flowers.

Amazu   "Sweet vinegar" in Japanese, amazu is used as a sauce, as a marinade, and in various ways in cooking.

Ankimo   Monkfish liver. When steamed, it has a texture similar to *foie gras* terrine.

Anticucho   Grilled bite-size pieces of meat on small skewers.

Asian pear   See *nashi*.

Bay scallops   Tiny, tender scallops, *Argopecten irradians*, from coastal waters.

Bay shrimp   See *Biscayne bay shrimp*.

Binchotan oak charcoal   Dense, almost pure carbon, binchotan retains temperatures up to 1800 °F (1000 °C). It burns with no flame and cooks food via infrared heat.

Bird's-eye chili pepper   Tiny but very hot chili pepper, a variety of *Capsicum frutescens*.

Biscayne bay shrimp   A pink shrimp from Biscayne Bay. Any bay shrimp can be substituted.

Black cod   An Alaskan fish, *Anaplopoma fimbria*, not actually related to cod, with rich but mild off-white flesh.

Black sea bass   An Atlantic coastal fish, *Centropristis striata*, mild, lean, and white-fleshed.

Bonito flakes   Bonito (skipjack tuna) fillets, steamed, dried, smoked, cured with a fermenting mold, and shaved like wood. Steep like tea in any liquid to add a rich, smoky taste.

Bottarga   The salted and dried egg sac of the striped mullet.

Branzino   Italian sea bass, *Dicentrarchus labrax*, with mild, lean, and white flesh.

Caigua   *Cyclanthera pedata*. Native to Peru, caigua (pronounced *kai-wa*) is a 4 in. (10 cm) to 8 in. (20 cm) long, soft, hollow, spongy cucumber with black seeds, eaten fresh in salads.

Calcium chloride   A powdered mixture of two calcium salts (calcium gluconate and calcium lactate) that produces a product rich in calcium. Used in conjunction with sodium alginate, it can turn drops of a liquid solution into caviar-like orbs of liquid encased in a thin membrane.

Cape gooseberry   An orange, sweet Peruvian tomatillo, *Physalis peruviana*, which is not actually related to the gooseberry.

Causa   Peruvian mashed potatoes.

Ceviche   Raw fish marinated in lime or lemon juice with olive oil and spices, served as an appetizer. A Central and South American specialty.

Chalaca   Chalaca refers the Peruvian port of Callao, famous for the dish *cholos a la chalaca*, mussels with Callao-style salsa.

Cherimoya   A fruit, 4 to 8 in. (10 to 20 cm) long, with smooth fingerprint-like markings on its green skin. The white flesh is sweet, juicy, and very fragrant. Contains hard black seeds.

Chili garlic sauce   Any commercial sauce made from a blend of fresh, roasted or dried chilies and garlic, sugar, salt, vinegar and other seasonings. *Sriracha* is a famous example.

Chimichurri   A parsley, garlic and olive oil sauce for grilled meats, originally from Argentina, but now popular all over Latin America.

Conch   A mollusk with a single, large, spiral shell, pronounced "conk," with tough flesh that needs to be tenderized before eating (see p. 116 for details). The true conch species within the genus *Strombus* vary in size; at Nobu Miami, relatively small farm-raised Queen Conchs are used.

Cubeb peppercorn   A tropical southeast Asian vine bearing spicy berry-like fruits. The dried, crushed peppercorns are used medicinally or in perfumes and are sometimes smoked in cigarettes.

Daikon   Plump, long, large white radish that is essential to Japanese cooking.

Dashi   Japanese stock often made from dried bonito flakes and *kombu*.

Dulce de leche   Sweetened condensed milk that has been cooked at a low temperature for hours so that its proteins turn brown and develop caramel-like flavors.

Edamame   Young, green, edible soybeans. Available fresh or frozen (pre-cooked).

Eel sauce   See *kabayaki*.

Fermented black beans (dou chi)   Chinese salt-preserved black beans, pungent and flavorful.

Flounder   A brown flatfish, *Pseudopleuronectes americanus*, with its eyes on the right side of its body.

Fluke   A dark brown flatfish, *Paralichthys dentatus*, with its eyes on the left side of its body.

Fresno chili   A conical pepper, 2 inches long and 1 inch in diameter at the stem end, green in the summer and red in the fall, similar in heat to the jalapeño, but with a thinner skin. Great for salsas.

Futomaki   A thick sushi roll filled with various ingredients such as egg, *kampyo*, cooked eel or cucumber wrapped in nori and cut into slices.

Gin-an   A sauce of *dashi* stock thickened with potato starch and seasoned with light soy sauce, used to add gloss and flavor.

Green tea powder   Powdered tea used in the Japanese tea ceremony, called *matcha* in Japanese. Very popular ingredient among European pastry chefs for adding a unique roasted flavor and green color.

Griot   A Haitian dish of pork cubes marinated overnight, boiled and then fried.

Grouper   A reef fish, *Mycteroperca bonaci*, with dark skin and a huge mouth, and mild white flesh.

Hajikami ginger pickles   Edible pickled ginger shoots, often used as a garnish to add a bright pink color to a dish.

Hamachi   Farm-raised yellowtail/amberjack, *Seriola quinqueradiata*, with fatty, meltingly soft meat.

Harumaki   Japanese spring rolls, fillings wrapped in a paper-thin wheat-based dough sheet and deep-fried.

Hatcho miso   A red miso, made from 100% soybeans and salt.

Hearts of palm   The inner core and growing bud harvested from certain edible palm trees, with a pleasant crunchy texture and sweetness like cooked fresh bamboo shoot.

Himalayan black salt, Himalayan pink salt   A mineral salt with a distinctive sulphurous smell.

Hoba magnolia leaves   The leaves of the hoba magnolia or Japanese umbrella tree (*Magnolia hypoleuca*), normally about 16 in (40 cm) long, used as a fragrant natural plate for grilled dishes.

Huacatay   A black mint-like herb, *Tagetes minuta*, native to Peru.

Jamón ibérico   A dry, salt-cured, aged Spanish ham made from the black Iberico hog, which is small, fatty and unique in that it seeks out and eats acorns, which give the ham a distinct flavor.

Japanese cucumber   A small, 8 in. (20 cm) long cucumber with a thin, edible skin, highly regarded for its crunchiness.

Japanese eggplant   A small eggplant, 5 in. (12 cm) long, with a thin skin and a delicate flavor.

Kabayaki   Food dipped in sweet soy sauce and grilled. Freshwater eel (unagi) is famous for being cooked kabayaki style. The sweet soy sauce is called kabayaki sauce.

Kabocha pumpkin   A Japanese winter squash. Kabocha has a dark green skin and bright orange flesh. Popular for its sweet, buttery flavor and fluffy texture when cooked.

Kampyo   A large round gourd from which long strips are planed and dried. The white dried strips are sold in a pack. Used for sushi rolls, they are simmered with fish broth, soy sauce and sugar until they become brown and tender.

Kanzuri fermented chili paste   Red chili pepper, frozen and dehydrated, then ground with *yuzu* skin, rice starter (*koji*) and salt, then fermented. Similar to *yuzu-pepper paste* but with a more fermented taste.

Kataifi   Shredded, noodle-like phyllo dough.

Key lime   A small, round, thin-skinned lime, *Citrus aurantifola*. Sharper tasting than the common Persian lime.

King crab   Not a true crab, this large crustacean, *Paralithodes camtschaticus*, has a spiny shell and long, spidery legs more than 3 feet (1 m) wide when extended. The meat is sweet, moist and rich.

Kinome leaves   Tender leaves of the *sansho* tree, used as garnish, chopped like an herb, or mixed into a paste with white miso.

Kinzanji miso   A fermented paste of barley, rice, wheat and vegetables, a Japanese condiment often eaten with sake or rice.

Kiwicha   A Peruvian staple grain, the seed of the amaranth (*Amaranthus caudatus*), high in vitamins and protein.

Kochujan   A spicy fermented paste of sticky rice, soybeans, and chili peppers from Korea.

Kombu   Dried giant kelp, used for adding meaty-tasting glutamic acid to dishes such as *dashi*.

Kudzu starch   A thickening agent made from kudzu root, often used in Japan. Kudzu starch hold its shape well and doesn't alter the flavor or color of the food.

Kumamoto oyster   A small, but plump and juicy oyster from Kumamoto Bay, on the southernmost island of Japan, Kyushu. The eggs were brought to the U.S. and are farm raised along the West Coast. Sadly, in Kumamoto they are almost extinct.

Kumquat   A small, oval orange-like citrus fruit, *Fortunella* spp., with a thin, sweet peel (generally eaten skin-on).

La you hot oil   Chinese hot oil made from the Chinese red chili pepper. Good la you hot oil is not only hot, but also very flavorful. Available in Asian food markets.

Long pepper   An elongated brownish-black fruit, *Piper longum*, encased in fleshy spikes, a close relative of black pepper, with a unique flavor and heat. They are used whole to flavor simmered meats, or may be ground and used like black pepper.

Lucuma   A round fruit with green skin and orange flesh, a staple in Peru used for ice cream, cake, juice and many other dishes. Its flavor is reminiscent of chestnuts and persimmons.

Lychee   A small fruit, 1½ in. (3 cm) in diameter, with a pinkish-red, pebbly rind. Only the translucent juicy and sweet flesh is eaten.

Lychee syrup   In Nobu restaurants, the syrup that canned lychee are packed in is used for cocktails. Just separate the syrup from the fruit.

Madako octopus   Eaten raw as sushi, or vinegared, simmered, braised and grilled, madako (*Octopus vulgaris*) is the most common octopus in Japan, with an average length of 24 in. (60 cm). It can be found throughout the world's warm seas.

Maui onion   A sweet variety of onion from Hawaii. Vidalia sweet onion is an acceptable substitute.

Minneola orange   Actually a tangelo, a cross between a grapefruit and a tangerine, this citrus fruit is large, sweet, juicy and fragrant, with a distinct bulge on the stem end.

Mirin   A sweet rice wine made from sticky rice, rice mold and usually additional distilled alcohol. Adds sweetness and sheen to cooked ingredients.

Miso   A strongly flavored paste made by fermenting soybeans and rice or barley with salt. An essential ingredient in the Japanese larder.

Mitsuba herb   An important Japanese herb which adds accents in flavor and crunch (from the stems).

Mojo   A flavorful Caribbean sauce made from olive oil, garlic, and red pepper.

Momiji oroshi   A mixture of grated daikon and red chili pepper. The name "momiji" means maple, as the vermillion color resembles maple leaves in the fall.

Mongo cuttlefish   Cuttlefish with a flavorful, moist and chewy texture. In Asian market look for "*banno*" (all-purpose) cuttlefish.

Mora berry   A red blackberry-like berry, *Rubus glaucus*, from the northern Andes.

Moromi miso   A fermented paste of soybeans and wheat, often eaten with raw vegetables, originally a byproduct of making soy sauce, but now usually made separately as a miso.

Nashi   A type of pear mostly eaten in Asia with a round shape and juicy, crunchy, coarse-textured flesh.

Nigiri-zushi   An oval, hand-formed nugget of sushi rice topped with a fish slice and grated wasabi.

Nori   A seaweed sheet made from pressed, dried and toasted algae. Regular nori sheets are about 8 ½ x 7 ½ in. (21 x 19 cm), usually sold 10 sheets to a pack.

Ocopa sauce   A creamy white sauce made from fresh cheese, *huacatay* (Peruvian mint), *ají amarillo*, garlic, and other spices.

Okiuto   A flavorful agar jelly made by sun-drying seaweed, then boiling and allowing it to firm up naturally. A breakfast staple in the Japanese Hakata region, where okiuto strips are eaten with bonito flakes, soy sauce and various vegetables.

Osetra   Eggs of the Ossetra sturgeon (at some point in history one "s" was lost from the name of the fish to the name of the caviar); one of the three elite varieties of caviar (the others are sevruga and beluga)

Pacojet   A Swiss-made machine that grates frozen foods to less than 0.1 mm in size, making a frozen purée or mousse. Very popular among European chefs for making frozen desserts from anything at all.

Panko   Japanese prepared breadcrumbs, available at many food markets.

Passion fruit   A tropical fruit ranging from yellow, red to purple outside with orange, jelly-like flesh surrounding edible seeds.

Peruvian corn   Peru actually grows more varieties of corn than anywhere else on Earth, but Peruvian corn usually refers to a type with large, pale-yellow kernels.

Peruvian pink salt   A pinkish-beige salt harvested from a salty spring in the Peruvian Andes.

Peruvian yellow potato (papa amarilla)   A flavorful potato grown in the Andes, less waxy than varieties grown in the lowlands.

Piklis   A Haitian side dish of cabbage cooked with vinegar and hot peppers.

Pink shrimp   A small shrimp, *Pandalus borealis*, which is red in color when alive.

Pomelo   A huge pale-green citrus fruit, *Citrus maxima*, larger and sweeter than a grapefruit, with a very thick spongy rind.

Pompano   A beautiful silver fish, *Trachinotus carolinus*, with distinctive long fins along the top and bottom rear edges of its diamond-shaped body. Rich, mild, tender but meaty, pompano is one the best eating fishes.

Ponzu   A dipping sauce made from citrus juice and soy sauce.

Poussin   A small, 1-pound chicken, also called a Cornish game hen.

Raw sugar   A tan, coarsely granulated sugar made from clarified sugar cane juice. True raw sugar is prohibited in the U.S., so the sugar labeled as "raw sugar" is somewhat refined.

Red miso   A miso made from fermented soybeans with little or no rice. Deep brownish-red in color with a rich fermented flavor.

Red mullet   A brilliant red and yellow fish, *Mullus surmuletus*, not related to true mullets, but actually a goatfish.

Red papaya   A special papaya from Mexico and the Caribbean with beautiful rose-red flesh and a juicy, tender texture.

Red rice vinegar   A richly flavored rice vinegar made from sake lees that have been fermented for three years. Traditionally used to make Tokyo-style sushi rice.

Renge   "Renge" means lotus flower in Japanese. It is a flat-bottomed, lotus-petal shaped table spoon used to eat soup, jelly or fried rice, especially throughout China and Southeast Asia.

Ribbon consistency   The consistency reached after beating, when the mixture poured from a height falls like a ribbon.

Ribeye cap   The thin muscle that covers the much more expensive ribeye muscle. Ask your butcher to provide it for you.

Rocoto   See *ají rocoto*.

Saikyo miso   White miso from Kyoto, fermented with more than twice as much rice as soybeans, which results in a salty-sweet beige paste.

Sake   A liquor made by a double fermentation of rice with rice mold (*koji*), yeast and water. In this book, sake from Hokusetsu is used for special dishes.

Salsa   A spicy sauce of chopped, usually uncooked vegetables or fruit, especially tomatoes, onions, and chili peppers, used as a condiment.

Sansho   A Japanese pepper tree, *Zanthoxymun peperitum*. Both the seeds and leaves are used is cuisine.

Sashimi   Very fresh raw fish, selected, prepared, sliced, and served with the utmost care, usually with pungent and refreshing garnishes.

Serrano chili pepper   Hot, rather small green or red pepper, one of the many varieties of *Capsicum annuum*.

Shari   Derived from Sanskrit "zaali," meaning rice. Refers to cooked vinegared sushi rice.

Shichimi spice powder   Spice mixture commonly made by mixing chili pepper powder, sesame seed, poppy seed, hemp seed, *sansho* pepper, dried orange peel and nori.

Shichirin   A portable cooking stove, for grilling or heating with charcoal.

Shishito pepper   Small, mild Japanese pepper typically deep-fried without batter (the skin is always pierced to prevent bursting.) Though a different size, Anaheim peppers are good substitute.

Shiso   A green or red leafy herb, *Perilla frutescens*, in the mint family, with a unique refreshing taste.

Shochu   See *soju*.

Siphon (with N₂O)   A bottle with a foam attachment that applies pressurized N_2O from a cartridge into the liquid in the bottle, transforming the liquid into a stable, airy foam.

Sodium alginate powder   This extract of seaweed is a cold gelling agent that is activated in the presence of calcium.

Soft ball stage   This stage occurs at 235–240 °F (112 to 115 °C) when cooking sugar syrup. This stage can be determined by reading a candy thermometer, or by dropping a spoonful of hot syrup into a bowl of ice water; if it has reached the soft-ball stage, the syrup easily forms a ball in the cold water. You can return the sugar ball to the pan.

Soju   A Korean distilled alcohol made from rice. Nobu Soju is made by Hokusetsu and has a distinct flavor, with the smoothness of sake and the punch of vodka.

Sour orange (Seville orange)   A rough-surfaced orange, *Citrus aurantium*, with a fairly thick and aromatic rind, too sour to be enjoyed out-of-hand, mostly used for making marmalade or orange oil. Its juice is used for sauces in Latin America, such as the Cuban *mojo*.

Spanish mackerel   A silvery fish with subtle black spots, *Scombero-morus maculatus*. Milder and richer than common mackerel.

Spiny lobster   Florida spiny lobster is a Caribbean variety of lobster, *Panulirus argus*, which lacks prominent claws.

Stone crab   A red-brown, rather smooth-shelled crab with black-tipped claws, *Menippe mercenaria*. Only one claw is harvested, and the crab is returned to the water.

Striped bass   Caught along the Atlantic coast of the United States, the striped bass, *Morone saxatilis*, has a silvery body marked with 6 to 8 longitudinal dark stripes. It has a moderately fat, firm-textured flesh with a mild, sweet flavor.

Superfine sugar   Finely pulverized granulated sugar with no addi-tives ("confectioner's sugar" has cornstarch added). Called castor sugar in Europe.

Tamari   A sauce made from soybeans with little or no wheat. Darker, and richer than soy sauce.

Tengusa sea tangle   A commercial product made from boiled ten-gusa seaweed formed into threads. It has a unique crunchy texture, like reconstituted jellyfish.

Tequila añejo   A distilled spirit made mainly in Tequila, Mexico from the blue agave plant, aged for at least a year (*añejo* means "aged").

Thermomix   The Thermomix is multi-cooking machine made in Germany that can be used as a blender, mixer, ice-cream maker, food processor, or a timer, hot pot and scale.

Tiradito   A Peruvian dish consisting of slices of raw fish dressed with ceviche seasonings. Its name is derived from *tirar* (the Spanish for "throw") because the fish slices are thrown into the serving bowl.

Toban   A flat earthenware pot which cooks food with mild and even heat.

Tobanjan   Tobanjan is the Japanese name for *dou ban jiang*, a Chi-nese fermented fava bean paste with red chili pepper.

Tobiko flying fish roe   The tiny salted eggs of the flying fish, often dyed orange, green, or gold with natural vegetable coloring.

Tomatillo   A tart, green fruit with a papery husk, *Physalis philadel-phica*, used in green salsas.

Toro   The fattiest part of the bluefin tuna, divided into *o-toro*, the fattiest tuna belly, and *chu-toro*, somewhat less fatty tuna belly.

Tosazu   Vinegar heated with bonito flakes, rich and smoky in flavor.

Udo   White herbal stalks, *Aralia cordata*, with a flavor similar to asparagus. Young stems can be eaten raw.

Udon   Thick noodles made with wheat, salt and water.

Umami   Found in some amino acids or other components in protein-rich food, this is "delicious" or "savory flavor." Ripe tomatoes, beef, aged cheese, mushrooms, *kombu* and dried bonito flakes are most famous for containing many umami components.

Uni   The reproductive organs of the sea urchin, orange in color, with a soft, buttery texture that melts in your mouth delightfully.

Uniq fruit   Also called ugli fruit, a knobby, mottled yellow and green tangelo (cross between a grapefruit and a tangerine) from Jamaica.

Vidrio   Chili peppers pickled in brine.

Wagyu   Although use of the name "wagyu" is strictly regulated by the Japanese government in Japan, in other countries, "wagyu" refers to beef with intense fatty marbling.

Wasabi   A pungent green horseradish, *Wasabia japonica*, which adds a refreshing and clean taste, especially to raw fish.

White miso   Miso made with briefly fermented soybeans and rice. Light brown in color and quite sweet.

Yamagobo pickles   Young shoots of *moriazami* (*Cirsium dipsac-colepis*), pickled in miso or soy sauce.

Yamamomo bayberry preserves Fruits of the bayberry or wax myrtle, eaten fresh, made into jam, or used for making liquor. Yamamomo preserved in shochu liquor for about 2 months is used as a condiment in Japanese *kaiseki* cooking.

Yuzu   An important citrus, believed to be a cross between sour man-darin orange and Ichang lemon. Yellow in winter and green in summer, yuzu is used to add a distinctive pungent, sour, citrusy taste to Asian dishes. Bottled juice may be available in Japanese grocery stores.

Yuzu-pepper paste (yuzu-kosho)   A commercial seasoning made from ground yuzu rind, hot green chili peppers, and salt.

ACKNOWLEDGMENTS

During the two weeks I stayed in Miami for the preparation of this book, it was difficult to concentrate on cooking, there were so many other things to do. But when I finally did get down to cooking, it was my first time working such long hours together with Thomas. Through the book production, he and I came to a deep understanding of one another. It was his first time making a cookbook. I know he learned a lot, and I'm sure the experience will prove a definite plus for him in the future.

To Daniel and Ferran, who wrote the forewords, and all our friends who gladly agreed to be quoted, my thanks. To George, who graciously gave us free use of his home again and again for our photo shoots, my grateful appreciation, as well as for the yacht and poolside, real Miami locations without which this just wouldn't be a party book. And of course, I mustn't forget to mention the many people who helped make all the necessary arrangements.

From the first meeting when I saw Taizo Kuroda's dishes taken out of their boxes, I felt compelled to go all out. To think that I could serve food on Kuroda's wares in a place like Miami was an honor in itself.

The photo sessions were hard work, but thanks to the uncompromising efforts of Kuma, the photographer, Miki, the art director and Noriko, the editor who came all the way from Japan, we pulled it off. The book looks great.

Lastly, to all the Miami staff and Bahamas staff who put up with me from morning to night, and to everyone in the Nobu Family involved in making this book, my heartfelt gratitude. With all my *kokoro* . . . *¡muchísimas gracias!*

Translation by Alfred Birnbaum, Derek Wilcox and Yamuel Bigio

Photograph on page 6 © Melanie Dunea
Photographs on page 190 © Steven Freeman

（英文版）NOBU マイアミ

2008年7月28日　第1刷発行

著　者　　松久信幸、トーマス・バックリー

撮　影　　久間昌史

発行者　　富田 充

発行所　　講談社インターナショナル株式会社
　　　　　〒112-8652 東京都文京区音羽 1-17-14
　　　　　電話　03-3944-6493（編集部）
　　　　　　　　03-3944-6492（営業部・業務部）
　　　　　ホームページ　www.kodansha-intl.com

印刷・製本所　大日本印刷株式会社